Tilde *skills*

Create Electronic Presentations

plus Challenges & Assessment Tasks

Microsoft PowerPoint 2013

Tilde Publishing and Distribution

Tilde *skills* Create Electronic Presentations
1st edition, 2nd printing

Author:
Tilde Publishing and Distribution

ISBN: 978-0-7346-0858-1 (print)
ISBN: 978-0-7346-2085-9 (ePDF)

Published by:
Tilde Publishing and Distribution
PO Box 72
Prahran VIC 3181 Australia
www.tilde.com.au

Ts-CreatePPT-PPT2013-1e2p

Contents

Preface vii
Topic 1 – Using presentation applications 1
Presentation technology 1
Before you begin 2
Terms & concepts review 3
Topic 2 – Getting started with PowerPoint 4
The Start Screen 5
Creating a new presentation from a theme 6
The PowerPoint screen 7
Exploring your presentation 10
Saving your presentations 11
Opening your presentation 13
Closing and exiting your presentation 15
Topic 3 – Slide basics 17
Using presentation themes 17
Choosing a slide size 19
Creating a blank presentation 20
Adding a new slide 21
Changing the layout of a slide 23
Checking your spelling 24
Formatting text and paragraphs on a slide 26
Changing the format of bullets and numbers 30
Previewing and printing your presentation 32
Previewing your work 32
Printing your work 33
Moving or copying text on a slide 35
Terms & concepts review 37
Topic 4 – Working with an entire presentation 38
Using the Slide Master 38
Adding a slide footer 40
Re-arranging your slides 41
Working in the Outline View 43
Topic 5 – Pictures, placeholders, shapes & tables 49
Inserting picture files 49
Manipulating your pictures 52
Working with placeholders 54
Inserting basic shapes 55
Inserting a table 58
Applying table styles, borders and shading 61
Topic 6 – Creating a chart 64
Charting with PowerPoint and Excel 64
Selecting a chart type 67
Editing your chart data 68
Topic 7 – Organisation charts with SmartArt 72
Creating an organisation chart 72
Changing the structure and layout of an organisation chart 73
Terms & concepts review 80
Topic 8 – Preparing notes, handouts & running your presentation 81
Adding speaker notes 81
Using the Handout Master to tailor audience handouts 83
Running your slide presentation (manually) 85

Annotating a slide show 86
Hiding slides 87
Topic 9 – Slide transitions & text/object animations 89
Using slide transitions 89
Adding text and object animations 91
Topic 10 – Rehearsing a presentation 96
Rehearsing and recording your timings 96
Setting the mode of your presentation 97
Topic 11 – Enhancing your pictures and photos 99
Enhancing your picture style 99
Adjusting your picture 101
Creating a Photo Album 104
Editing your Photo Album 106
Enhancing your Photo Album 106
Terms & concepts review 108
Topic 12 – Completing your skills 109
Importing a text outline 109
Creating a custom show 110
Creating an agenda/summary slide using hyperlinks and custom shows 112
Packaging a presentation for a CD 115
Skills challenges & Assessment tasks 117
Creating a working area 117
Appendix I - Shortcut keys: Direct key combinations 127
Shortcut keys: PowerPoint 2013 access keys 128
Appendix II – Additional topics 129
Customising the Quick Access Toolbar 129
Using Help 129
Index 131

Preface

Introduction

This publication can be used as a tutorial for self-paced learning or for instructor-led teaching. Its purpose is to enable students to prepare and produce electronic presentations, using Microsoft PowerPoint 2013. If kept conveniently near your computer it can also be used as your primary reference, reminding you of the most efficient ways to approach your presentation tasks.

Business Services Training Package

The contents of this publication can contribute to achieving the following unit of competency in the Business Services Training Package: *BSBITU302B Create electronic presentations*.

Pre-requisites

The following pre-requisites or equivalent knowledge apply:

Be Competent in Operating a Personal Computer and/or
Be Competent in Using Business Technology.

Performance criteria - Business Services Training Package
Unit BSBITU302B Create electronic presentations

1. **Prepare to create presentation**
    1.1. Organise personal work environment in accordance with ergonomic requirements
    1.2. Determine purpose, audience and mode of presentation in consultation with content author or presenter
    1.3. Identify presentation requirements in terms of supporting documents, transparencies and equipment
    1.4. Apply work organisation strategies and energy and resource conservation techniques to plan work activities
2. **Create presentation**
    2.1. Design slides, notes and handout masters to incorporate organisational and task requirements in relation to image and preferred style, avoiding distractions
    2.2. Use software functions for consistency of design and layout, to meet identified presentation requirements
    2.3. Balance presentation features for visual impact and emphasis
    2.4. Use advanced software features to streamline and customise the presentation for different audiences
    2.5. Prepare presentations within designated time lines
3. **Finalise presentation**

3.1. Use manuals, user documentation and online help to overcome problems with design and production

3.2. Check presentation for spelling, consistency in presentation features and style, in accordance with task requirements

3.3. Print presentation materials in accordance with presenter or audience requirements

3.4. Store presentation, in accordance with organisational requirements and exit the application without information loss or damage

How this publication is organised

This publication contains **12** topics. Each topic contains: concept overviews; detailed **How to** explanations; and abundant **Hands-on** exercises.

Consolidation tasks are used at intervals to bring skills together. These tasks can be undertaken by a student on his or her own, or as a team review in the classroom.

At the rear of the course, **Skills challenges** and **Assessment tasks** are included. Skills challenges are undertaken by a student on his or her own, and provide further practice and challenges. **Assessment tasks** are suitable to assess competency in the unit.

Information contained in the **Appendices** can be brought into the course at any time. Certainly **Help** can be studied whenever further information is sought.

Tilde conventions

The following conventions are used throughout Tilde publications.

Convention explained	Example
Each topic begins with an overview of relevant theory (a narrative). In narratives, important terms are shown in **bold**.	'PowerPoint has many built-in **themes** that...'
Narratives are often followed by examples or useful additional information (an aside).	***For example …*** ***As an aside …***
A set of **How to** steps follows a narrative. These steps detail the procedure required to perform a task. These can be read by a student, presented by a trainer, or referred to when using the manual as a reference.	**How to: Save a new presentation** 1. ... 2. ... 3. ...
A command button is shown beside the relevant **How to** step, and often as a reminder in **Hands-on exercises**.	
In **How to** steps, names of command buttons are highlighted in **bold**. Steps also include the name of the ribbon where the button is located, and the group.	'Display the View ribbon, then click on the **Slide Master** button (Presentation group).'
Pictures of keys are used to illustrate keys on the keyboard.	Ctrl Enter

An exercise to be undertaken by a student is called a **Hands-on exercise**. Each exercise step is described in detail and is used to practise and reinforce the skill being learned.	**Hands-on exercise X**
In exercises, file names are shown in *italics*. Key actions are also highlighted in bold.	**'Open** the presentation *Health centre*.'
Additional useful **Hints & tips** are used to help students apply their skills more successfully, overcome problems and extend their knowledge.	
Terms & concepts review questions are used to review key terms and concepts covered in a topic.	
To review or consolidate student skills a **Consolidation task** is used. This task can be undertaken by a student on his or her own, or as a team review in the classroom.	**Consolidation task X**
To help students apply their new skills in realistic scenarios a work-based task called a **Workplace scenario** is used.	

How to use this publication in a self-paced manner

Read through the **How to** step(s), and then work through the following **Hands-on** exercise.

Accompanying exercise files are required to work through the exercises. These can be downloaded from the Tilde website <www.tilde.com.au>, or obtained from the publisher. It is recommended that they are pre-loaded into a suitable folder on a hard drive (e.g. My Documents), or a network drive.

How to use this publication in an instructor-led classroom

Present to students the material in the **How to** steps; then, have them work through the **Hands-on** exercises.

Accompanying exercise files are required to work through the exercises. These can be downloaded from the Tilde website <www.tilde.com.au>, or obtained from the publisher. It is recommended that they be pre-loaded into a suitable folder on a hard drive (e.g. My Documents), or a network drive. Exercise files can be freely copied onto student PCs, instructor PCs, or network drives when used for education purposes with a Tilde™ publication.

Spelling

The Macquarie dictionary is used except for the names of features from the application, e.g. Center Align, where the original (American) spelling is used.

Instructor email list

To be notified regularly of new educational developments from Tilde Publishing, go to the Tilde Publishing website www.tilde.com.au.

The Tilde *skills* series

This publication is just one in the Tilde *skills* series that addresses the educational needs of adults in the workplace. It is suitable for anyone wishing to learn using Tilde's enjoyable methodology.

Another Tilde imprint for the business services training package is Tilde *business.* These books integrate the latest educational material with the outcomes of the national curriculum. Each Tilde *business* publication is education, accessible, and affordable.

For more information on Tilde *skills* or Tilde *business,* please visit our website www.tilde.com.au.

Before you start

To ensure you get the best results from this course please check the settings have been set from the previous student for a fresh installation of Microsoft Office 2013.

Downloaded with the student exercise files is a PDF file used for reference within the course. Please print out the following file for your students before course commencement: *OH&S guide.*

A note about operating systems

This course was written using Microsoft Office 2013 running on Windows 8. If your personal computer or network is running a different operating system, e.g. Windows 7, you may notice some differences. These differences will be minor and are unlikely to affect the course content and exercises. The differences will most likely be noticed in relation to Taskbar operation and navigation within Save As and Open dialogue boxes.

New to Office 2013

Office 2013 suite of programs incorporates many new features in terms of its interface and the functionality it provides. You can configure many of these software features by selecting Options from within Backstage view and locating the appropriate section. More information can be found by searching on the specific aspect within Help.

Depending on the setup of your network or personal computer, as a user of Office 2013, you may have the option to 'sign in' using a Hotmail account when you use the software. Once signed in, you can use the SkyDrive to save and access files. SkyDrive is a Cloud-based storage feature that enables you to store and access files from multiple devices.

Topic 1 – Using presentation applications

When preparing a presentation, the use of visual aids can help to emphasise your message and make it easier for your audience to understand and retain the information presented.

Today's range of presentation software allows you to create sophisticated presentations that are clear, easy to understand, and visually impressive.

> *Examples of presentation applications include: Microsoft PowerPoint; Adobe Presenter 7; Open Office Impress.*

In this course you use Microsoft PowerPoint to create attractive, professional-looking presentations.

Presentation technology

There are a number of ways you can elect to display your presentation. The method you select will depend on the size of your audience.

For one or two people, the audience can simply gather around your computer or laptop. For larger audiences there are better options. Connecting your computer to an electronic projector will enable you to present to large audiences in big auditoriums For presentations being held in a meeting room or in a classroom you can use printed overhead transparencies on an overhead projector, connect your computer to an LCD projection panel that sits on top of an overhead projector, or connect to an electronic whiteboard. Presentations can also be printed on paper, or a photographic bureau can take your output and create 35 mm slides.

Electronic projector

LCD projection panel
(Liquid Crystal Display)

> ***As an aside** ...PowerPoint 2013 also lets you easily design presentations for use on the internet, particularly useful when your audience is spread around the country or the world.*

Before you begin

Before you begin any presentation, you must define your target audience.

> ***For example ...** Is your presentation intended for general office staff or for members of the board of directors?*

To ensure a clear, appropriate and captivating presentation, learn what you can about your target audience and consider how your message might be read.

Also consider the mood of your presentation, conservative, factual, easy-going, shocking, humorous, etc.

Tips for making your presentation look good

- Ensure your presentation has structure, with an introduction, a body, and an end.
- Avoid using general slide titles like Overview or Introduction. Use titles that will mean something to your audience.
- Restrict the text on your slides to the main points only. Avoid using paragraphs of text. Twenty words - or six lines of text - is generally the maximum recommended per slide.

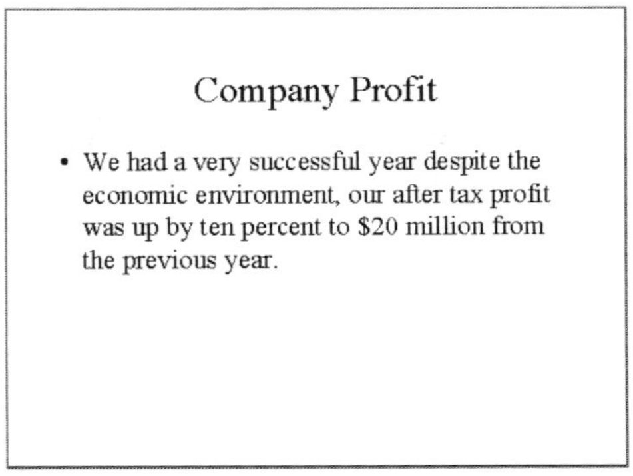

Avoid large paragraphs of text

- Avoid the use of too many fonts, font sizes or attributes on one slide, i.e. don't use bold, italic and underline on the same slide.
- Ensure font size is not too small for audience to read.
- Choose your font colours carefully – ensure they separate clearly from the slide background.
- Write your points using lower case letters. Don't write all in UPPERCASE, as this slows down the rate at which people can read your points.
- If you are unsure about the font itself or the size and colour you selected, stand at the back of the room and let the presentation run to see how legible the text is.
- Where possible, use pictures or diagrams rather than words to illustrate your points.

- Avoid putting too many small pictures or drawings on one slide, as this is confusing to the eye. Use one large picture instead.
- Ensure your slide background is not overly busy.
- Don't use unnecessary special effects (irrelevant animation, overuse of sound, too many transitions) – content rules!

Terms & concepts review

- What are the 3 main points to remember before you begin your presentation?

  1)

  2)

  3)

- How do you structure your presentation?

  1)

  2)

  3)

- What are some ways to ensure your presentation can be easily understood?

  ____

  ____

  ____

  ____

  ____

  ____

Topic 2 – Getting started with PowerPoint

PowerPoint provides a variety of ways to create and view your slides using different layouts, designs and formatting.

Starting PowerPoint

When you start PowerPoint a new blank presentation is displayed ready for you to commence your tasks.

How to: Start PowerPoint Windows 8

1. From the Start Screen, click on the **PowerPoint** button.

How to: Start PowerPoint Windows 7

1. Click on the **Start** button. The **Start menu** is presented.
   Click on

Or, if PowerPoint is not in your list of recently used programs …

From the **Start menu** type: 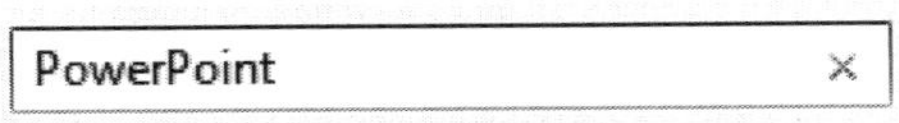

Microsoft PowerPoint will be presented in your list of **Programs**.

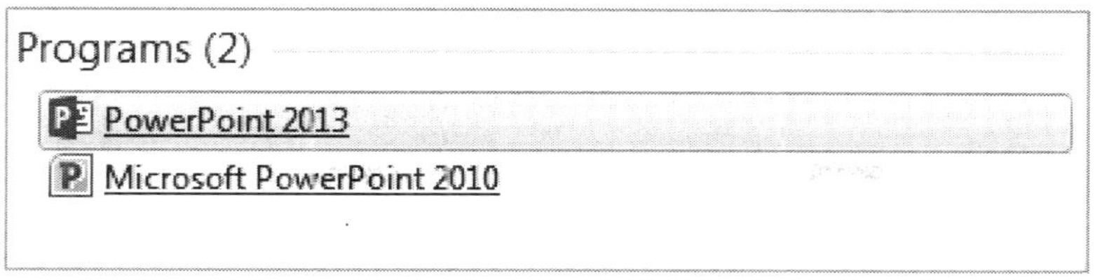

Note: some computers may still have Office 2010 still installed (if you are working from a home computer, when you install Office 2013 from the internet, it does not uninstall 2010).

1. Press Enter to start the selected program.
   PowerPoint's **Start Screen** will appear.

The Start Screen

The **Start Screen** is new to PowerPoint 2013. The Start Screen provides access to recently used files, PowerPoint templates and blank presentations.

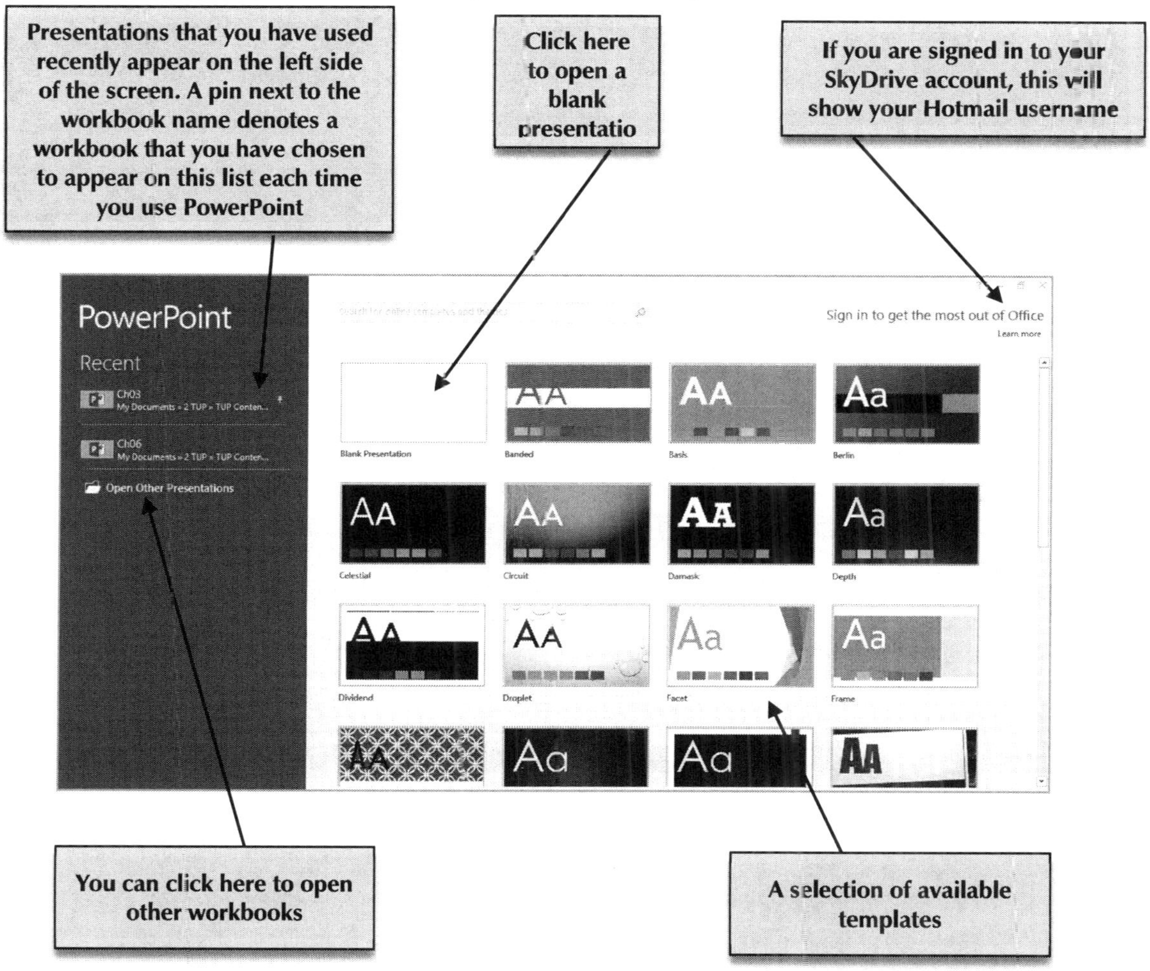

If you have signed into SkyDrive, you will see options for additional templates and themes under the search bar.

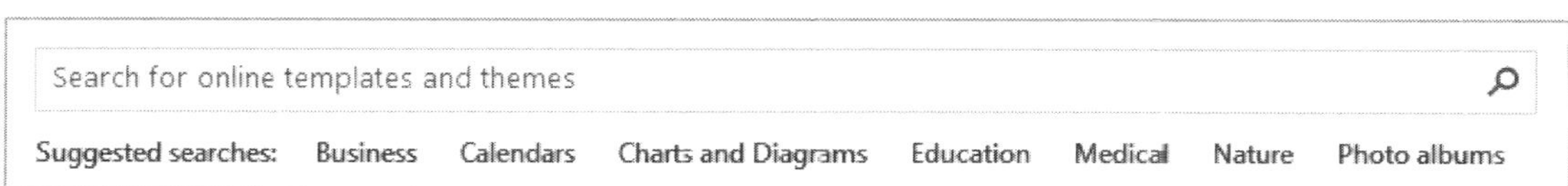

Creating a new presentation from a theme

When you open PowerPoint you have the option to create a blank presentation or to start from a pre-designed theme. These themes give you more guidance and ideas to set up your presentation.

How to: Create a new presentation using a theme from the Start Screen

1. **Start** PowerPoint.
2. In the available themes, click on a theme.
3. PowerPoint then offers you a larger preview of the theme from the start screen.

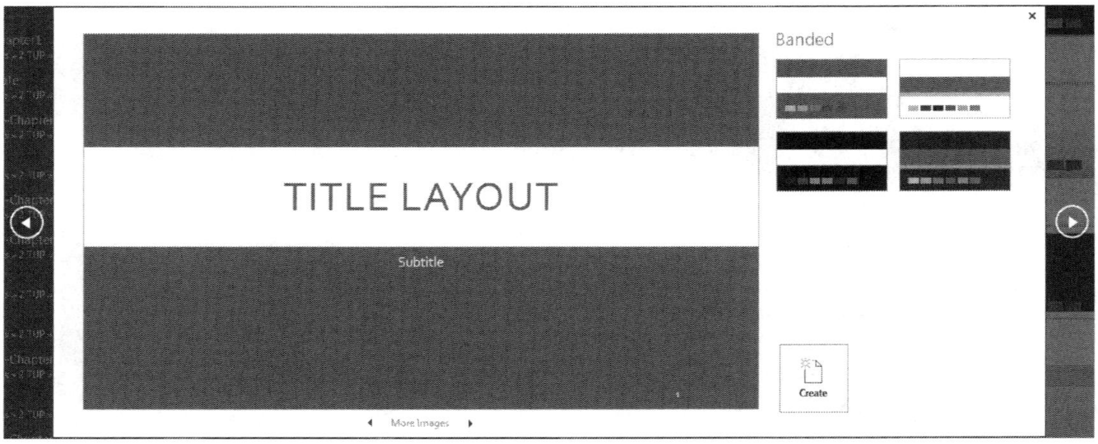

4. Using the large arrows on the left and right of the window, scroll through to see more theme previews.
5. To see more images of the selected PowerPoint, click on **More Images** under the large preview.
6. Click on **Create.**

As an aside *... You can search for more themes and templates online by typing a keyword into the search box at the top of the Start Screen. You need to sign into your SkyDrive with a Hotmail address to access these additional themes and templates.*

Hands-on exercise 1

In this exercise you will practise starting PowerPoint and creating a presentation from a pre-designed theme.

- Read your printout of the *OH&S guide* supplied with your student exercise files and check your workstation setup. Refer to the Preface (Before you start) if this document is not available to you, or ask your instructor.
- Start PowerPoint (see instructions above for Windows 7 or 8)
- Click on the **Ion** theme from the selection presented.
- Scroll though **More Images**.
- Click on the **blue** colour scheme.

- Click on **Create**.
  A new presentation is produced from the selected theme.
- Leave your *'Ion'* presentation open on the screen.

The PowerPoint screen

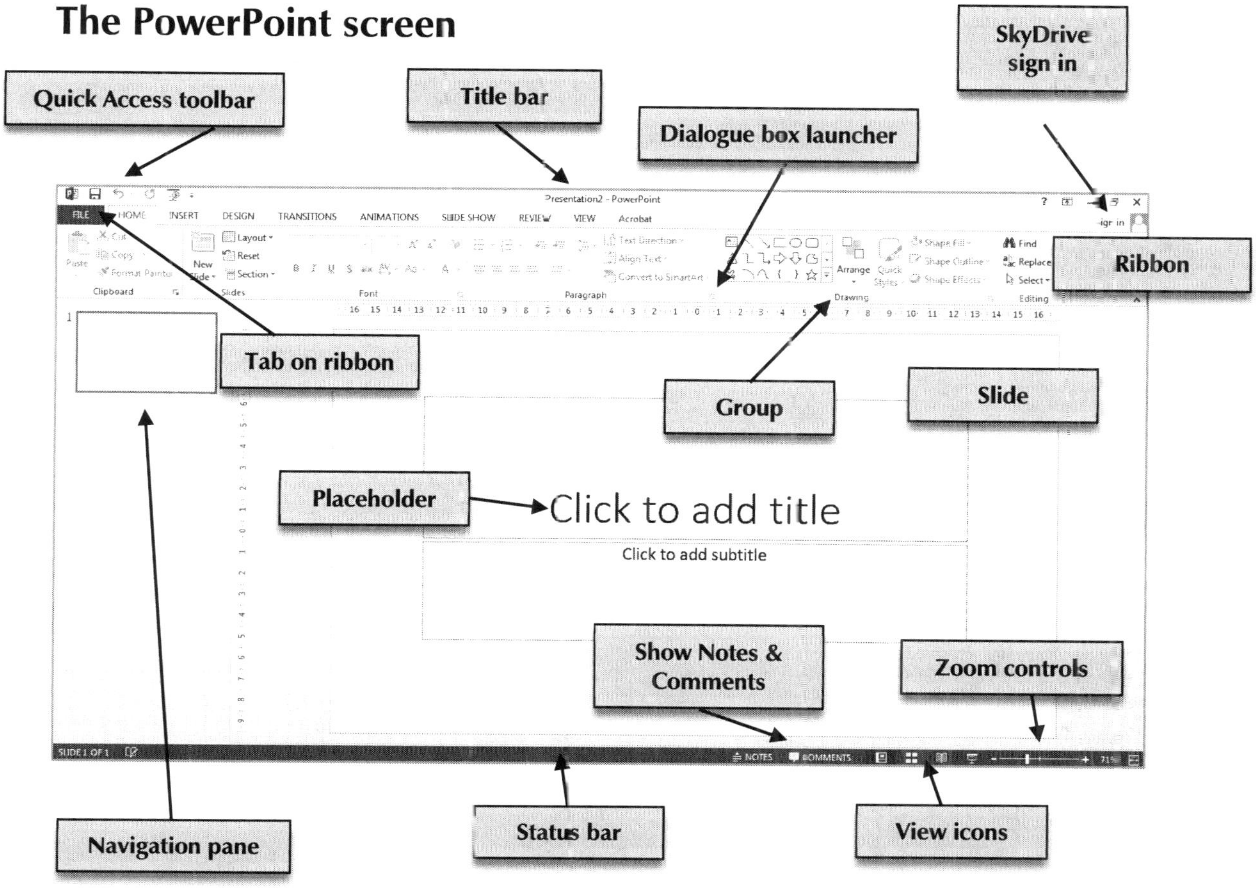

Quick Access toolbar	A toolbar which contains a set of commands which can be added to and used as your personal collection. The basic commands are Save, Undo and Redo.
Title bar	Indicates the name of your current presentation (Presentation1), and the application name (Microsoft PowerPoint).
Ribbon	Ribbons house your command buttons. Each ribbon represents a type of activity. For example, the Home ribbon has all your basic commands, e.g. add a new slide and format text. The Insert ribbon gathers together objects you can insert such as pictures, tables and shapes. Certain ribbons only appear when needed. If you point to a command button on a ribbon without clicking on it, a ScreenTip displays a description of the button.
Tab	Each ribbon has a tab displaying its name. Click on a tab to display a ribbon.
Group (of commands)	The commands on each ribbon are organised into groups, e.g the Home ribbon, Slides group.
Dialog box launcher	Some groups have a Dialogue box launcher which opens a dialogue box of further commands (downward-facing arrow in bottom-right of group).

Slide	Every PowerPoint presentation consists of slides. Within each slide are dotted boxes called **placeholders** that hold text, pictures and other objects. The arrangement of text, pictures, charts, and other objects on a slide is called a layout.
Navigation pane	Displays slide thumbnails or a text outline of your presentation, as it develops.
Notes and Comments	Use to type notes to accompany each slide, e.g. reminders of points to make when presenting. These do not appear on the screen when you deliver your presentation, but they can be printed.
Status bar	Indicates the status of your presentation, e.g. slide number/number of slides in presentation, design theme, dictionary in use. It also displays any messages that you receive, e.g. when saving a presentation. You can right-click on the Status bar to see a list of items that can be added to the bar.
View icons	Indicates your current view and allows you to move between views. The default view is Normal view.
Zoom controls	Use to enlarge or reduce the magnification level of your slides.

Hints & tips

The ribbon can be minimised to show just the tabs (useful on a laptop). Double-click on any tab. Double-click again to restore. The ribbon still re-appears as needed (click on a tab), then disappears when not needed (click back in presentation or outside of the ribbon).

Displaying Backstage view

Backstage view is accessed by clicking on the **File** tab. Backstage view brings together actions for managing your documents, particularly creating/opening and finishing your presentations. Actions on other ribbons relate more to changing the content in your presentation.

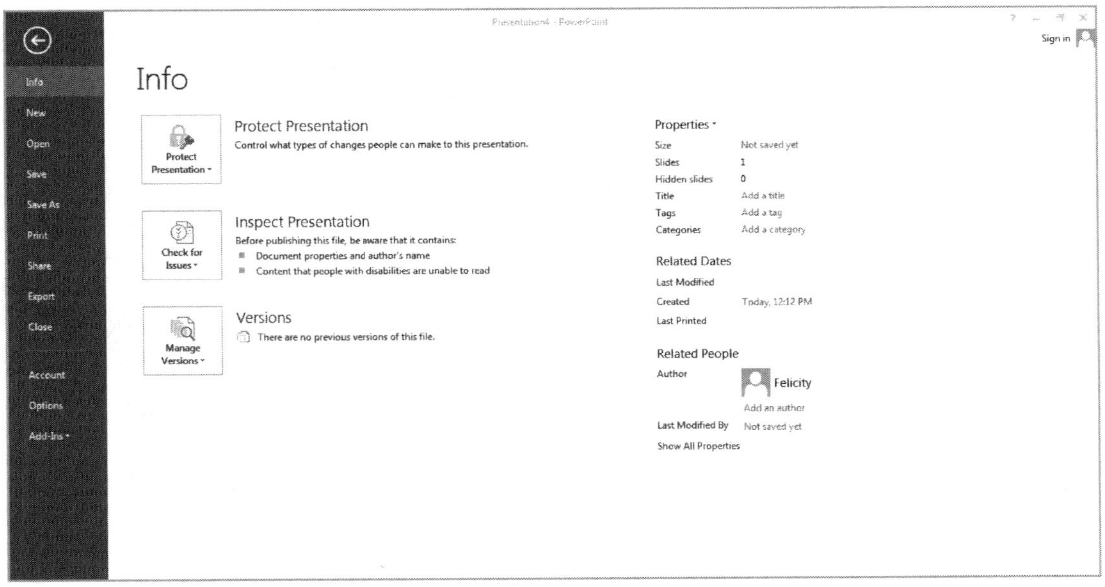

Hands-on exercise 2

In this exercise you access Backstage view.

- Using your presentation from the last exercise, click on the **File** tab. Backstage view is presented. Note the actions that can be selected from the left panel, e.g. Save, Open, Close, New, Print.
- Click on **New** and you will notice it shows the templates from the Start Screen.
- Click on Info. How many slides does it say the current presentation has? ____________________
- Click on the **arrow** to exit Backstage view, or press Esc. You return to where you were originally working.

You need to be signed into your SkyDrive to complete the rest of this exercise.

- Click on the **File** tab, then click on **New**.
- Click in the search box at the top of the new screen.
- Type the word: marketing
- Click on the magnifying glass or press Enter. Numerous templates and themes on this topic are presented (**Search results**).
- Click on **Marketing plan presentation**, then click on **Create**.

- The template will download automatically, then the presentation is displayed.
- Leave your presentations open for the next exercise.

Exploring your presentation

Next, you discover the variety of views you can use to navigate through your presentation.

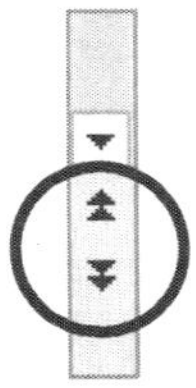

How to: Move between slides (Normal View)

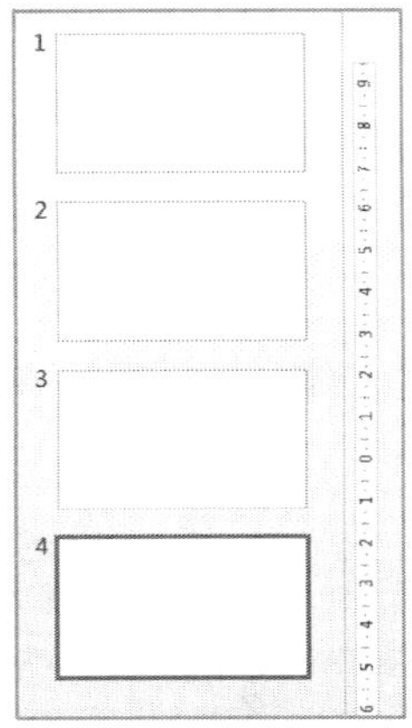

1. Click on the **Next Slide** or **Previous Slide** buttons located at the base of the vertical scroll bar (to the right of the slide).

~or~

1. With your mouse over the active slide, scroll down to the next slide and scroll up to the previous slide.

~or~

1. Click on the required slide on the Navigation pane.

Keyboard shortcuts *can often save you time and effort and are used in place of commands from the ribbon. (Keyboard shortcuts are illustrated throughout this text and can also be found in Appendix I.)*

Action	Keys
Up one slide	Page Up
Down one slide	Page Down
To move quickly to the first slide	Ctrl Home
To move quickly to the final slide	Ctrl End

Hints & tips

If a slide is displayed too large, click on the ***Fit Slide*** *button.*

How to: Select a different view

1. Click on the required **View icon** (see far right of Status bar)

~or~

1. Display the View ribbon and click on the required button (Presentation Views group).

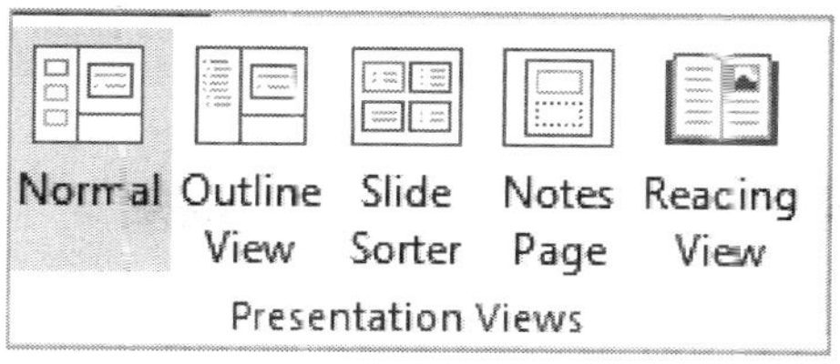

Presentation views

Normal	The default view. Simultaneously displays the slide, navigation pane and notes pane.
Outline View	Outline view allows you to view and work on slide text without any colour, pictures or formatting.
Slide Sorter	Displays all the slides of your presentation. This makes it easier to select a slide, and then move, copy or delete it.
Notes Page (View ribbon)	The current slide is presented with the Notes area below.
Reading View	Allows you to view your presentation as a slide show within the window.

Saving your presentations

Until you save a presentation, it exists only in the computer's short-term memory. To save a presentation you need to supply a file name and a storage location (drive, library/folder). A storage location is initially selected for you (the default storage location), but you can easily select another location.

Windows allows file names up to 255 characters in length, including spaces. A number of characters are invalid, (i.e. they cannot be used for file names). These include: ? : * " \.

Choose file names that easily identify the presentation content. Organisations may set their own standards for file names, e.g. date, department, description, author.

How to: Save a new presentation

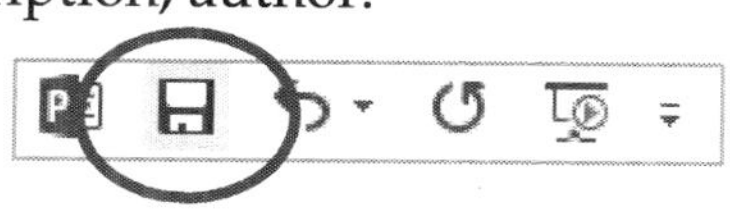

1. Click on the **Save** button (Quick Access Toolbar)
   ~or~
   Display **Backstage** view, then click on **Save As**
   The Save As screen is presented.

2. Choose a **destination** for your presentation (on the SkyDrive or on your computer – you may need to ask your teacher/supervisor if you are doing this course in a classroom).
3. Choose a folder in the **Current Folder** or **Recent Folders** list.
   ~ or ~
   Click on the **Browse** button and navigate to the required folder by clicking on a folder or other location in the left panel of the Save As dialogue box (**Navigation pane**).

   The current folder will be shown in the Address Bar at the top of the dialogue box.

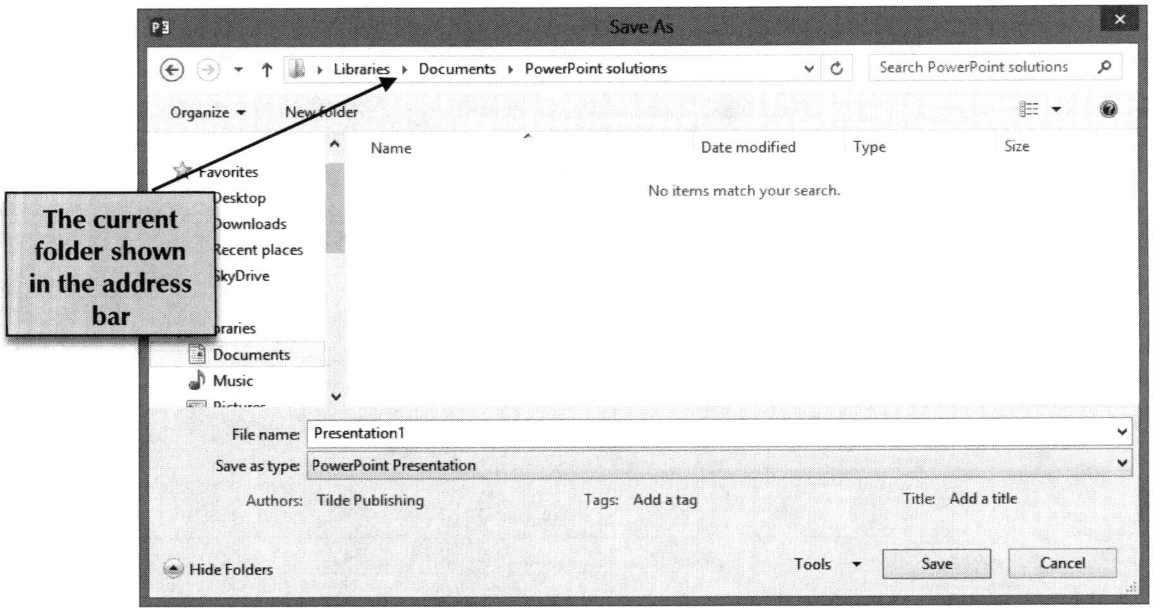

4. Type a **File name**.
   Your typing replaces the highlighted text which is only a suggestion.
5. To select an alternative storage location, click on a folder or another location in the panel on the left of the dialogue box (**Navigation pane**)
6. Click on **Save**.
   A Save message appears briefly in the Status bar.
   The presentation name then appears in the Title bar at the top of the screen.

How to: Save changes to your presentation

1. Click on the **Save** button (Quick Access Toolbar).
   The previously saved version of the presentation is overwritten by the displayed version.

How to: Save a copy of your presentation

1. Display **Backstage** view, then click on **Save As**.
2. Select the destination, and locate the folder.
3. Complete the dialogue box with a new name.

	Save presentation	Ctrl S
	Save As	F12

__As an aside__ ...PowerPoint 2007, 2010 and 2013 all share the same file format, but earlier versions use a different file format. If you have a colleague who is working on an earlier version of PowerPoint, you will need to save your presentation in compatibility mode (PowerPoint 97-2003 Presentation).

Opening your presentation

How to: Open a presentation once PowerPoint is started

1. Display **Backstage** view, then click on **Open**.
   The Open screen is presented.

2. If your presentation has recently been opened, it will be displayed in **Recent Presentations**, otherwise select the storage destination.
3. Select either a **Recent Folder** or click on **Browse**.
   The **Open** dialogue box is presented.
4. To select an alternative storage location within the dialogue box, click on a folder or other location in the panel on the left of the dialogue box (**Navigation pane**).
5. To select your presentation, double-click on the file name
   ~or~
   Click on the file name, then click on **Open**.

How to: Open a presentation from the Start Screen

1. Start **PowerPoint.**
   PowerPoint's Start Screen is presented.
2. Select a **Recent** presentation from the list

   ~or~

   Click on **Open Other Presentation** on the left panel.
   The Open screen appears.

3. If your presentation has recently been opened, it will be displayed in **Recent Presentations**, otherwise select the storage destination.
4. Select either a **Recent Folder** or click on **Browse**.
   The **Open** dialogue box is presented.
5. To select an alternative storage location within the dialogue box, click on a folder or other location in the panel on the left of the dialogue box (**Navigation pane**).
6. To select your presentation, double-click on the file name
   ~or~
   Click on the file name, then click on **Open**.

Open a presentation

Hands-on exercise 3

In this exercise you open and explore the variety of PowerPoint views and navigate through a presentation.

- Find out from your teacher/instructor where you should save your presentations (or use the **Documents** location).
  You may want to write down the location for reference.

  ____

- **Open** the presentation from your student supplied files: *Market brainstorming*.
- Display the View ribbon, then click on **Slide Sorter** button (Presentation Views group). Multiple slides are displayed.
- Double click on slide number 3 (notice the numbers to the left under the thumbnail) .
  This will open slide 3 in Normal view.
- At the base of the scroll bar, click on **Previous Slide** to move back to slide 2.
- Using your keyboard, move to slide 1 (Page Up).
- Click on the **Reading View** button (Status bar icon).
  Your presentation is launched within the window.
- Click to progress to the next slide in the show. (This will be discussed in more detail later in the book.)
- Click through all the slides
  ~or~
  Press Esc to stop the show.
- Click on the **Outline View** button. What is different in this view?

  ____

  ____

- Use the scroll bar to the right of the navigation pane to move down the outline text.
- Place your mouse over the splitter bar, your mouse will change to a double headed arrow.
- Click and drag your mouse to the right to widen the navigation pane.
- Click back on **Normal.**
- Display your *'Ion'* presentation.
- Show the backstage view, then click on **Save As**.
- Navigate to the folder you are to save in.
- Replace the file name with: **Induction quiz show**
- Leave your presentations open on the screen.

Closing and exiting your presentation

How to: Close a presentation

1. Display **Backstage** view, then click on **Close**.
2. If you have already saved your work the presentation closes immediately.
   If you have not saved your work you are prompted to save.

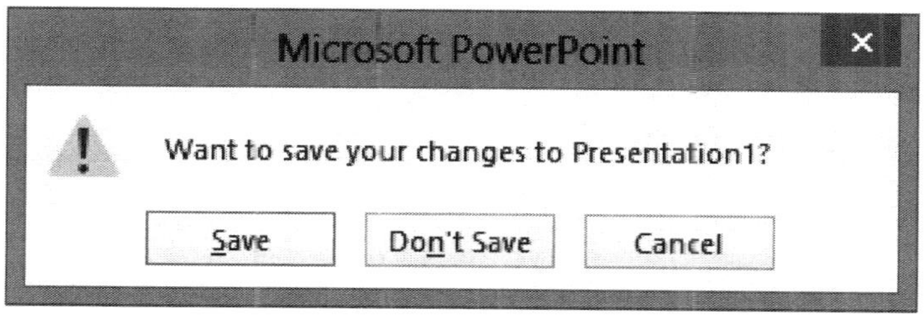

3. Click on **Save** to save your changes.
   Click on **Don't Save** to close the presentation without saving your changes.
   Click on **Cancel** to go back to your presentation.

***As an aside** … You can also click on the **Close** button in the top-right corner of your screen. However, if this is your only open presentation this also closes PowerPoint.*

Close a presentation

How to: Exit PowerPoint

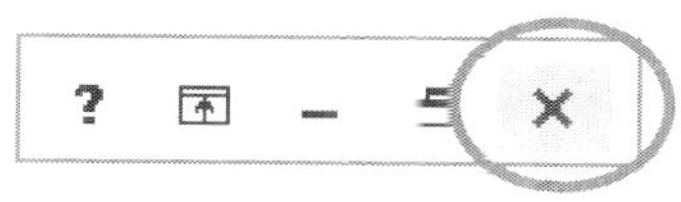

1. Click on the close button on the top right of your screen.
2. If you have already saved your work, PowerPoint and any presentations you have open close immediately. If you have not saved your work, you are prompted to save each un-saved presentation before the application can close.

Hands-on exercise 4

In this exercise you practice saving and closing your presentation.

- Ensure *Market brainstorming* is on your screen.
- Display the backstage view, click on **Close.**
  Notice, your other two presentation(s) are still open.
- With your *'Ion'* presentation on your screen, display the backstage view.
- Click on **Open**.
- Your *Market brainstorming* presentation should be in **Recent Presentations.** Single click on the presentation to open it.
- Display your *Induction quiz show* presentation.
- Using the close button on the top right, close your presentation.

- Display *Market brainstorming*.
- Using shortcut keys, close your presentation (Ctrl W).
- If you were able to sign in to complete Hands on exercise 2, **save** your presentation with an appropriate name.
  Try using shortcut keys (F12).
- Exit PowerPoint.

Topic 3 – Slide basics

Using presentation themes

PowerPoint has many built-in **themes** that consist of a set of colours, fonts and background styles. These themes can be applied to an existing presentation or can be used to begin a new presentation.

For example ... *A slide can look very different when a different design is applied.*

Banded theme

Slice theme

The theme you select will initially apply to all slides in your presentation, even if a new slide is added later.

As an aside ... *Use themes with dark backgrounds to make slides easier to read in your presentation. White or light backgrounds are better for overheads.*

How to: Apply a theme to an existing presentation

1. Display the Design ribbon, point to any option in the Themes group to see its name and the design effect previewed on your slide. Click on the **More** arrow to display the full gallery of themes.
2. Click on the required theme to apply.

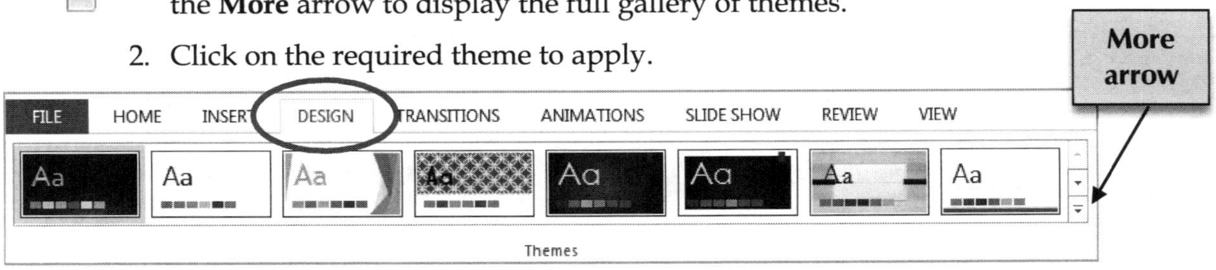

Similar to starting a presentation from a theme which you learnt in the last topic, you can choose a different variation (Variants) from the standard colour scheme.

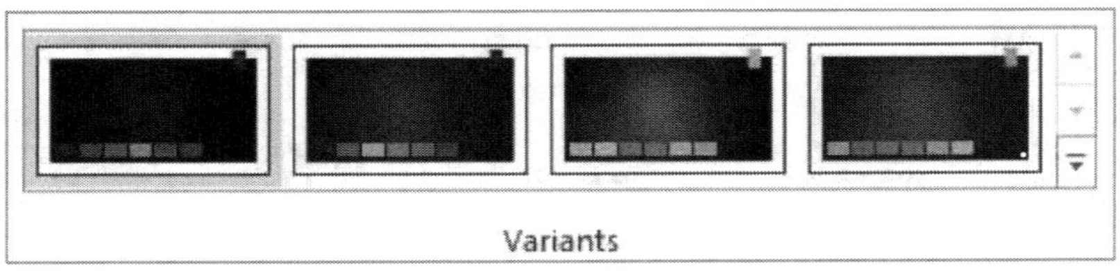

Hands-on exercise 5

In this exercise you practise using themes.

First, you apply a theme to an existing presentation.

- **Open** the presentation *Market brainstorming*.
- Display the Design ribbon, point to any option in the Theme group to see the design effect previewed (may take a few seconds to appear). Click on the **More** arrow  to display the full gallery of themes.
- Click on a theme of your choice.
- View your presentation in **Slide Sorter** view. Note that all the slides have the new design applied.
- Return to **Normal** view and display slide 1.
- View your presentation in **Reading View** to see the full effect on your slides.
- **Save** your presentation.

Next, you create a new presentation with a theme.

- Display **Backstage** view, then click on **New**.
- Double-click on a theme of your choice.
- Choose a colour variation if you want.
- Click on **Create**.
  A new presentation is produced using your selected theme.
- **Close** *Market brainstorming*.
- Leave your new presentation on the screen for the next exercise.

As an aside … You can fine tune themes by selecting the ***Colors****,* ***Fonts****, or* ***Effects*** *buttons on the Design ribbon (Variants group).*

Choosing a slide size

By default, presentations are sized for widescreen (16:9) as most of the televisions being sold are widescreen. However, slide setup can be altered to allow for other presentations (for overhead projector slides, A4 presentations etc.). **Slide size** should be set in the early stages of creating a presentation to retain correct positioning of objects.

Some slide sizes to note:

- On-screen Show (4:3) - standard
- On-screen Show (16:9) - widescreen presentation (default)
- 35mm Slides
- Overhead

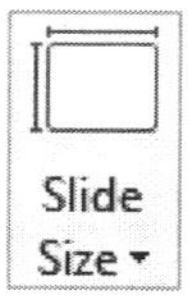

How to: Change your slide size

1. Display the Design ribbon, then click on the **Slide Size** button (Customize group).
2. From the drop down selection, click on **Custom Slide Size...** The Slide Size dialogue box is presented.

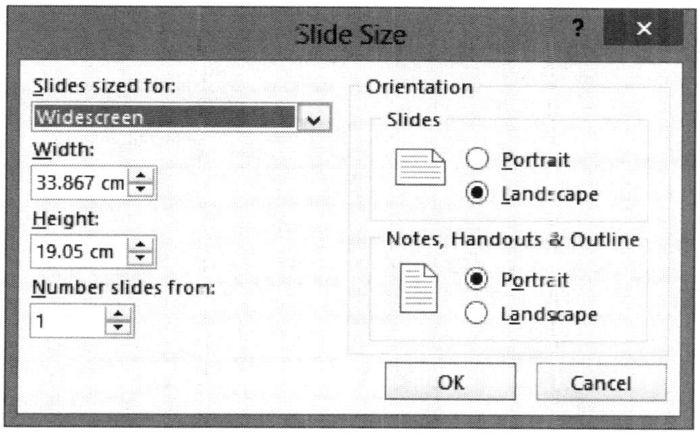

3. Click on the **Slides sized for** down-arrow, then click on the required size.
4. Click on **OK**.
5. To rescale your theme, click on **Ensure Fit**.

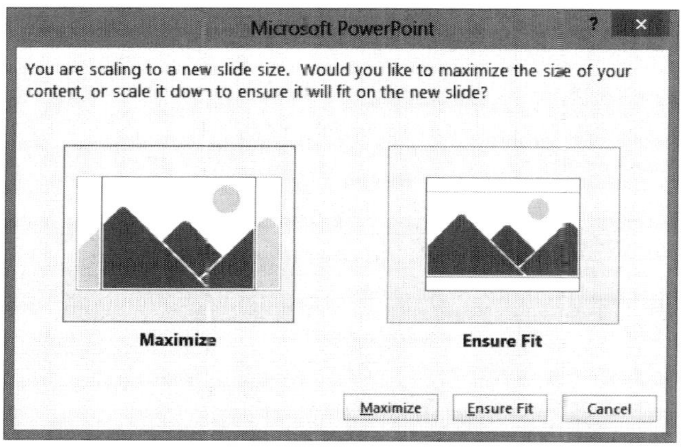

Hands-on exercise 6

In this exercise you practise changing your slide configuration.

- Using your new presentation from the previous exercise, display the Design ribbon.
- Click on the **Slide Size** button (Customize group).
- From the drop-down, click on **Custom Slide Size...** The Slide Size dialogue box is presented.
- Click on the **Slides sized for** down-arrow, then click on **A4 Paper (210x297 mm)**.
- Click on **OK**.
- To ensure your presentation is rescaled to the new size, click on **Ensure Fit**.
- **Save** your presentation as *A4 presentation*.
- **Close** your presentation.

Creating a blank presentation

From the Start Screen, you can choose to start a blank presentation and customise your fonts, colours and themes.

How to: Create a blank presentation

1. Start PowerPoint, then select **Blank Presentation**

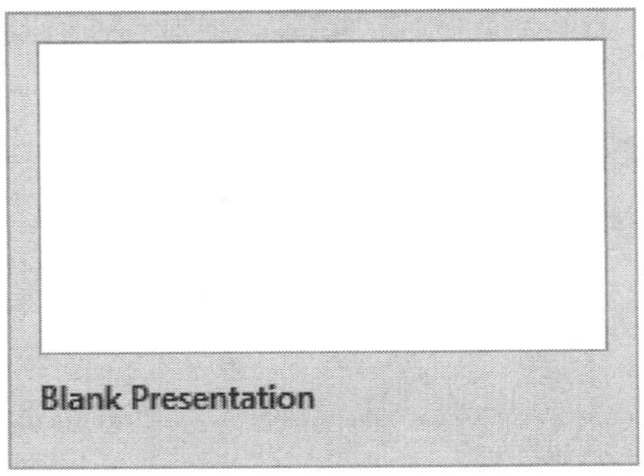

~or~

If PowerPoint is open, display **Backstage** view, then click on **New**.

2. Click on **Blank Presentation**.

> ***As an aside*** *... Commands you use often can be added to the Quick Access Toolbar. See Appendix II.)*

Hands-on exercise 7

In this exercise you practise creating a new blank presentation.

- Display **Backstage** view, then click on **New**.
- Click on **Blank Presentation**.
- The blank slide contains two placeholders (boxes with dotted lines) for your slide title and subtitle text.

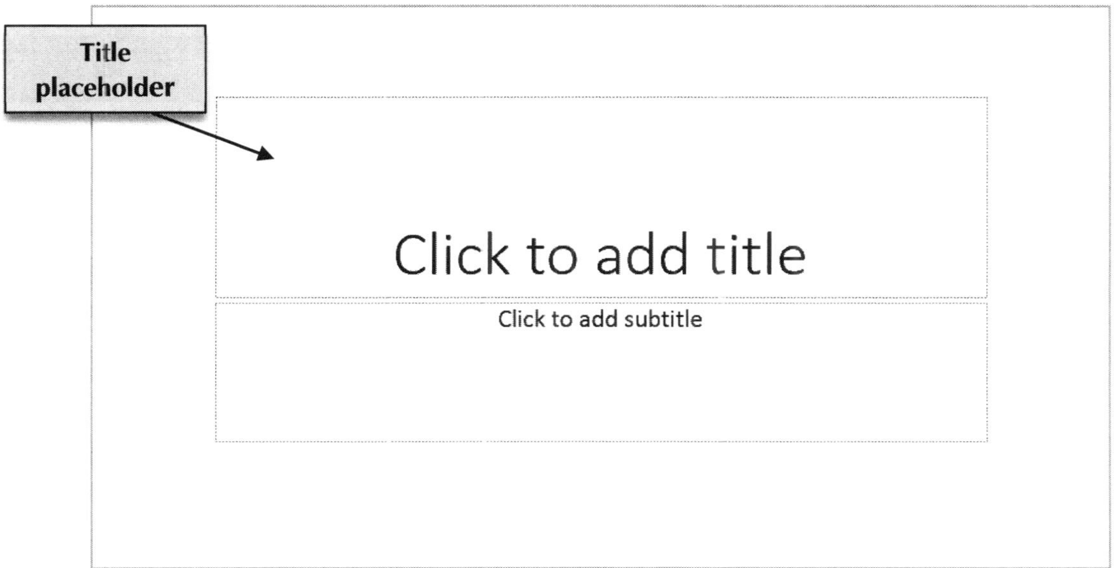

- Click on the title placeholder. The default text is removed.
- Type the new text: Home Security Hints
- Click on the subtitle placeholder. Type the new text: By Your Name
- Ensure your presentation is configured for a **Widescreen (16:9).**
- **Save** your presentation as *Home security*.

Adding a new slide

You can quickly add a **new slide** to a presentation. PowerPoint has one predefined layout for a Title Slide and eight for regular slides, e.g. Title and Content layout, Section Header layout, Two Content layout.

How to: Add a new slide

1. Display the Home ribbon, then click the top half of the **New Slide** button (Slides group).
   A new slide is added after the displayed slide with a default layout.

~or~

1. To select a layout, click the bottom half of the **New Slide** button (Slides group).
   A drop-down list is presented.

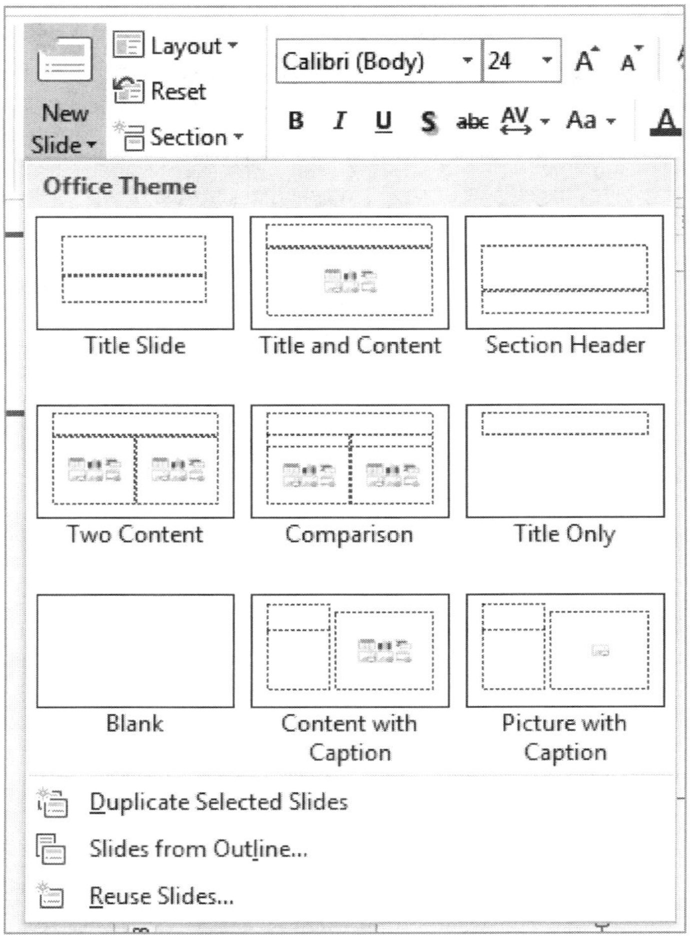

2. Click on a layout required, e.g. Title and Content. A new slide is added with the chosen layout.

As an aside *...You can also insert a new slide form the Insert Ribbon, Slides group.*

Hands-on exercise 8

In this exercise you practise adding a new slide to your presentation.

- Using the presentation *Home security*, display the Home ribbon.
- Click on the top half of the **New Slide** button (Slides group).
  A new slide is added after the displayed slide with a default layout (Title and Content).
- Click in the title placeholder, then type: First Steps
- Click in the text placeholder.
- Type: Make your home appear occupied
  Press Enter
- Type: Install outside sensor lights
  Press Enter
- Type: Don't leave newspapers outside
- **Save** your changes.

Changing the layout of a slide

You may find that you want to change the position or **layout** of content on a slide. Each slide contains placeholders that mark the position of a text and content. Content can include text, a picture, a diagram, a chart and a table You can select from a variety of different slide layouts.

How to: Change the layout of a slide

Layout ▾

1. Display the Home ribbon, then click on the **Layout** button (Slides group). A drop-down list is presented.

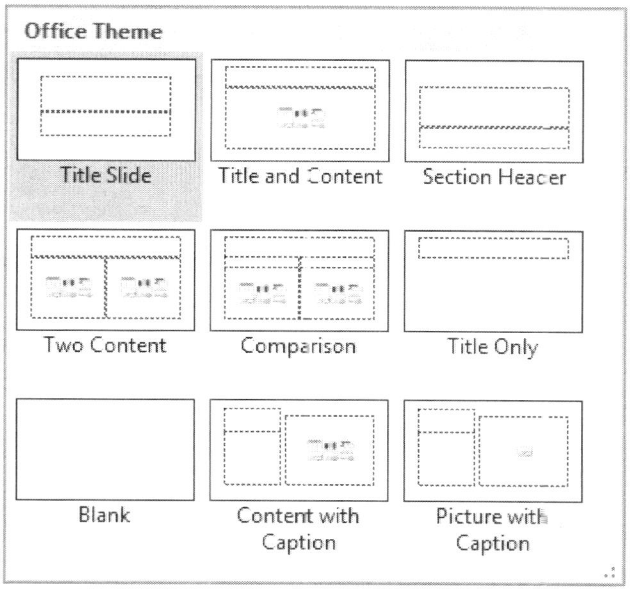

2. Click on the required layout. The slide displays the new layout.

*As an aside … Click on the **Undo** button (Quick Access toolbar) to remove an unwanted new layout. Use **Undo** to reverse most unwanted actions.*

Hands-on exercise 9

In this exercise you practise adding a slide, changing slide layouts and applying a theme.

- Using the presentation *Home security*, display the Home ribbon.

First, you add a new slide.

- Ensure you are on slide 2.
- Click on the bottom half of the **New Slide** button (Slides group).
  A drop-down list is presented. Click on the **Two Content** option. A new slide is presented with the selected layout.
- Click in the title placeholder, then type: Home v. Office Security
- Click in the first text placeholder, then type the following points pressing Enter after each new line: (Include the 3 deliberate spelling mistakes.)

  Improve your home securety
  Don't leave groceries on the doorsteep

Install window locks
Install a burgllar alarm
Install door chains

- **Save** your changes.

Next, you change the layout of a slide.

- Click on the **Previous Slide** button to display slide 2: First Steps.
- Click on the **Layout** button (Home ribbon, Slides group). A drop-down list is presented. Click on the **Two Content** option. The layout changes.

Finally, you apply a theme to your slides.

- Display the Design ribbon, point to any option in the **Theme** group to see the design effect previewed.
- Click on a theme of your choice.
- View your presentation in **Slide Sorter** view.
- Click on slide 1, then run your presentation in **Reading View**.
- Return to **Normal** view.
- **Save** your changes.

Checking your spelling

PowerPoint can help you check and correct **spelling** in your slides. Spelling errors are underlined with a red wavy line.

How to: Check your spelling

1. Display the Review ribbon, then click on the **Spelling** button (Proofing group).
2. When a spelling error is encountered, the Spelling pane will be displayed on the right of the screen.
3. Click on the required option.
4. When the spell check is close the pane by clicking on the top right close button.

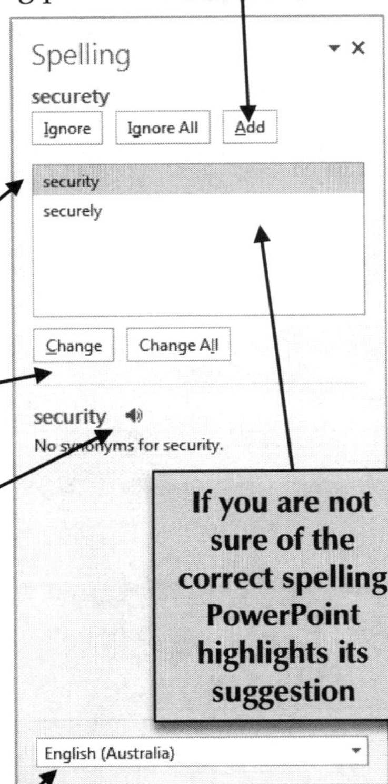

> ***As an aside*** *...You may notice some of your common typing mistakes are corrected for you as you type, e.g.* ***teh*** *corrected to* ***the*** *(when you press the Spacebar). This is called AutoCorrect. Typing mistakes that cannot be corrected automatically are underlined with a red wavy line.*

Hands-on exercise 10

In this exercise you practise checking your spelling.

- Using the presentation *Home security*, display the Review ribbon.
- Click on the **Spelling** button (Proofing group).
- Check your spelling and make any necessary changes.
- **Save** your changes.
- **Close** your presentation.

Hands-on exercise 11

In this exercise you practise creating a new blank presentation, then adding extra slides. You have been asked to create a four-slide presentation to accompany the launch of a new gardening magazine.

- Create a new blank presentation.
- Click on the title placeholder and type: Gardens Illustrated
- Click on the subtitle placeholder and type:
  A New Gardening Magazine
- Display the Home ribbon, then click on the top of the **New Slide** button (Slides group). A new slide is added after the displayed slide with a default layout (Title and Content).
- Click in the title placeholder and type:
  We're Leading the Way
- Click in the text placeholder, then type the following text pressing Enter after each line:
  Monthly guide to jobs in the garden
  Designed for the novice gardener
  Benefiting the local gardening industry
- Add another new slide (Title and Content).
- Click in the title placeholder and type:
  Our Sales are Growing
- Add another new slide (Title and Content).
- Click in the title placeholder and type:
  How to Buy Gardens Illustrated
- Click in the text placeholder and type:
  Available on the 1st of each month in your local supermarket

Ask for it to be ordered in to your local newsagency

Available at most large nurseries

Available directly from our website

To order a copy, contact Jackie at Gardens Illustrated

- **Save** your presentation as *Gardens illustrated.*
- Display the Review ribbon, then click on the **Spelling** button (Proofing group). Check your spelling.
- Display the Design ribbon, point to any option in the **Theme** group to see the design effect previewed.
- Apply the theme **Basis**.
- Click on slide 1 and view your presentation in **Reading View**.
- Return to **Normal** view.
- **Save** and **close** your presentation.

Formatting text and paragraphs on a slide

When you apply a **theme** PowerPoint selects formatting for your text and bullets. You can modify these selections.

> ***As an aside*** *...Changes made to text are considered to be exceptions and are not altered when a theme is applied or changed.*

How to: Apply character formats

1. Select the text to be formatted. (To select all the text in a placeholder, click in the placeholder then press [Ctrl] [A].)
2. Display the Home ribbon, then click on the required button (Font group). Multiple effects can be applied, e.g. bold and a font colour.

Calibri (Body) ▾	**Font** Click on the down-arrow to select a font for the text.
24 ▾	**Font Size** Click on the down-arrow to select a font size for the text.
A˄ A˅	**Increase Font Size** and **Decrease Font Size** Click to increase/reduce font size. Click and click again to increase/decrease more.
(Clear Formatting button)	**Clear Formatting** Click to remove all character formatting.
B *I* U	**Bold, Italic, Underline** Click for a basic bold, italic or underline.
S	**Text Shadow** Click to add a shadow behind the selected text.
~~abc~~	**Strikethrough** Click to add a line through text. Use to indicate text to be removed.

AV	**Character Spacing** Click to increase/reduce the spacing between characters. Choose from a drop-down list.
Aa	**Change Case** Click to change capitalisation. Choose from a drop-down list.
A	**Font Color** Click to change the colour of your text. Click on the down-arrow to select a colour.

Hints & tips

To make your slides easier to read, keep body text larger than 18 points and avoid using hard to read fonts, UPPERCASE or underlining.

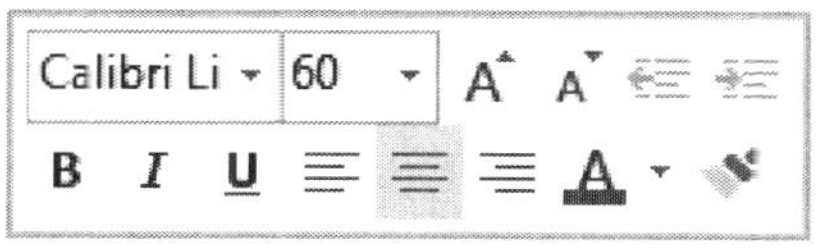

When text is selected you may see a semi-transparent mini toolbar alongside the selection. The toolbar is semi-transparent until you point to it. It disappears when you point away from it. In the following sections although the command buttons are documented from the Home ribbon, use of the mini toolbar is equally efficient, and can be useful as it is placed nearer your text.

Hands-on exercise 12

In this exercise you practise applying formatting to a presentation.

- Create a new blank presentation.
- Click in the title placeholder and type:
  How to bake cupcakes
- Press Ctrl A to select all the text in the placeholder.
- Change the font to **Arial Black**.
- With text still selected, increase font size by one.
- Click in the text placeholder and type:
  By Tested and True Cooking
- Press Ctrl A then apply **Italics.**
- **Save** your presentation as *Baking cupcakes.*
- Add a new slide (Title and Content).
- Click in the title placeholder and type the following:
  Ingredients
- Select the word *Ingredients* and change the case to **UPPERCASE**.
- While still selected, click on **Bold**, then change the **Font Color** to dark blue.

- Click in the text placeholder, then type the following text pressing Enter after each line:

  125g butter – melted
  2 eggs
  1 teaspoon vanilla essence
  ½ cup milk
  1 cup sugar
  1 ½ cups S.R. flour

- Press Ctrl A then change the font size to **36**.
- Add new slide (Title and Content).
- Click in the title placeholder and type:

  Method

- Create the same formatting for *Method* as you did for *Ingredients*.
- Click in the text placeholder, then type the following text pressing Enter after each line:

  Beat all ingredients by hand or electric beaters.
  Place a spoonful of mixture into greased patty pans.
  Cook 180 Degrees Celsius for 10-15 minutes.
  Decorate as desired.

- Press Ctrl A then change the font size to **36**.
- Apply the theme **Banded**, change the Variants to black and white (3rd colour in the variants group).
- Check your spelling.
- View your presentation in **Reading View**.
- Return to **Normal** view.
- **Save** your presentation.

How to: Apply paragraph formats

1. Select the text to be formatted. (To select all the text in a placeholder, click in the placeholder then press Ctrl A.)
2. Display the Home ribbon, then click on the required button (Paragraph group).

Button	Description
	Bullets Click on the button for the default bullet style, or click on the down-arrow for alternatives.
	Numbering Click on the button for the default number style, or click on the down-arrow for alternatives.
	Decrease List Level Decrease the indent level.
	Increase List Level Increase the indent level.

	Line Spacing Alter your line spacing.
	Align Left Align text to the left.
	Center Align text to the centre.
	Align Right Align text to the right.
	Justify Aligns text to both left and right, adding extra space between words as necessary.
	Columns Split a text placeholder into 2 or more columns.
Text Direction	**Text Direction** Rotate your text.
Align Text	**Align Text** Select how text is aligned within the text placeholder, e.g. align to the bottom of the placeholder.
Convert to SmartArt	**Convert to SmartArt Graphic** Display the selected text using a graphic, e.g. a pyramid or a Venn diagram.

Hands-on exercise 13

In this exercise you practise applying formatting.

- Create a new blank presentation.
- Change the layout of the first slide to **Title and Content**.
- Click in the title placeholder and type: *Discover the Flinders Ranges*
- Click on the **Center** button.
- Press [Ctrl] [A] to select all the text in the title placeholder.
- Click on the **Increase Font Size** button.
- With text still selected click on the **Character Spacing** button, then click on **Very Loose**.
- With text still selected click on the **Shadow** button.
- Click in the text placeholder and type the following pressing [Enter] after each line:

  Amazing scenery
  Deep gorges and soaring mountains
  Our world famous Ridges Tour
- Press [Enter] then click on the **Increase List Level** button.
- Type the following three points:

Lunch with eagles
Swim in crystal clear waterholes
2 billion years in the making

- **Save** your presentation as *Flinders ranges.*
- Select the word 'eagles' and apply **Bold**.
- Select the word 'waterholes' and change its **Font Color** to a dark blue.
- Apply the theme **Slice**.
- Click in the text placeholder and press Ctrl A to select all the text in the placeholder.
- Click on the **Increase Font Size** button.
- With the text still selected, click on the **Line Spacing** button, then click on **1.5**. Change the text colour to light blue.
- Click on the last point: *2 billion years in the making*. Click on the **Decrease List Level** button. (Ensure the font size is the same as the top 3 points.)
- Click on the **Align Text** button, then click on **Top**.
- **Save** your presentation.

As an aside *…When adding text to a slide, if you try to enter more text than can fit into a placeholder, PowerPoint tries to shrink the text to fit. If PowerPoint tries to shrink the text an* ***AutoFit Options*** *button appears beside the text. Point to the button and click on the down-arrow for options, Consider rethinking your text or starting another slide.*

Hands-on exercise 14

In this exercise you practise adding bullets and numbering to your presentation.

- Using the presentation *Baking cupcakes*, display slide 2 then click in the text placeholder.
- Select all the text in this placeholder then click on the **bullets** to remove the bullets.
- Display slide 3 and select all the text in the text placeholder Click on **Numbering**.
- Review your presentation, **save** your changes and **close** your presentation.

Changing the format of bullets and numbers

The appearance of **bullets** and **numbering** can be altered to add more appeal to your presentation.

How to: Change your bullets or numbers

1. Select the text you want to change the bullets or numbering. If it is the whole placeholder, then press Ctrl A.
2. Display the Home ribbon, then click on the **Bullets** or **Numbering** down-arrow (Paragraph group). Make a selection or click on the

Bullets and Numbering option. The Bullet and Numbering dialogue box is presented.

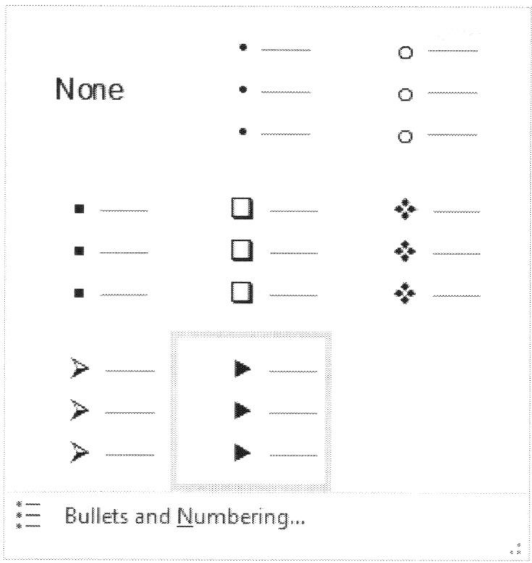

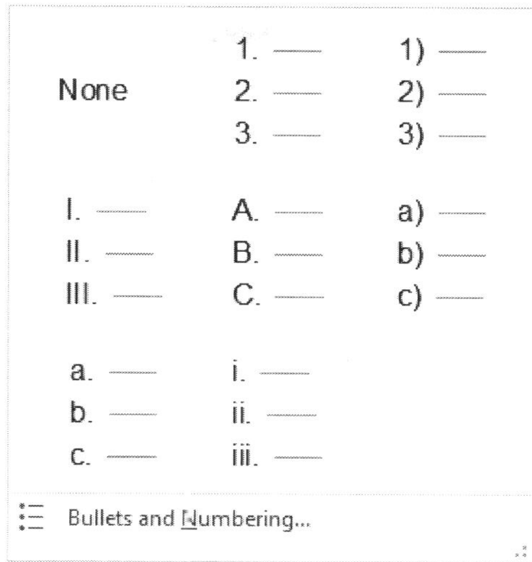

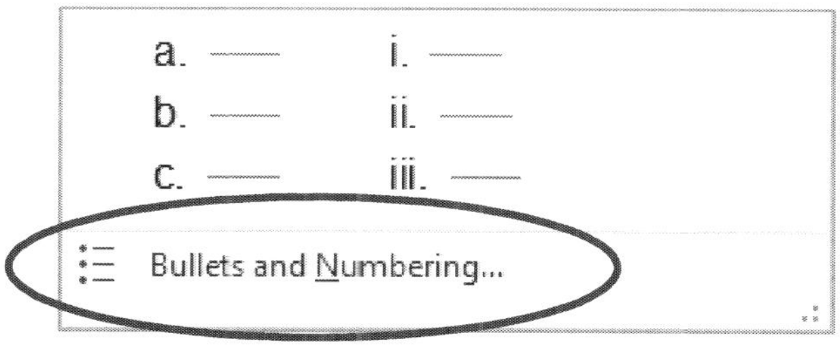

3. Select the **Bulleted** tab or **Numbered** tab.

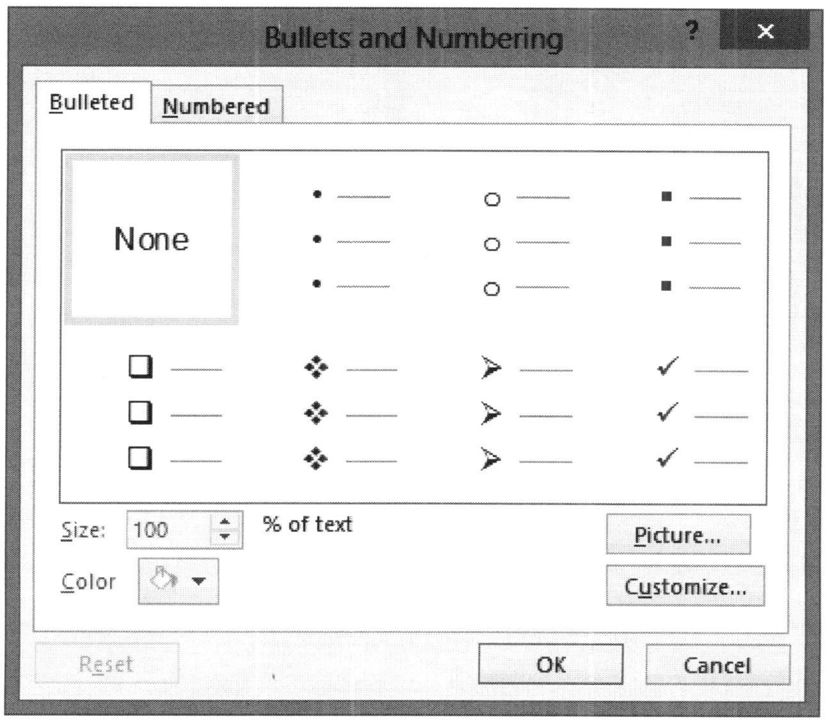

4. Change the **Size**, **Color** or **Picture** for your bullets.
5. Click on **OK**.

As an aside *... Deselect the Bullets or Numbering button to remove a bullet point/number against an item.*

Hands-on exercise 15

In this exercise you practise making formatting changes to bullets and numbers.

- Using the presentation *Flinders ranges*, click in the text placeholder and select all of the text in the placeholder.
- Click on the **Bullets** down-arrow, then click on **Hollow Round Bullets** from the list presented.
- Click on the **Bullets** down-arrow again, then click on the **Bullets and Numbering** option. The Bullets and Numbering dialogue box is presented.
- Set the bullet size to 95% and select a dark blue colour.
- Click on **OK**.
- Select the two bullet points at a lower level (drag over text to select).
- Click on the **Numbering** button.
- Keeping the text selected, click on the **Numbering** down-arrow, then click on the option **a. b. c**.
- Keeping the text selected, click on the **Numbering** down-arrow again, then click on the **Bullets and Numbering** option. The Bullets and Numbering dialogue box is presented.
- Set the number size to 85%.
- Click on **OK**.
- Select the two bullet points at a lower level, and press .
- **Save** and **close** your presentation.

Previewing and printing your presentation

PowerPoint makes the process of generating printouts easy. In PowerPoint 2013 you preview and print in the **Print Place** in Backstage view.

Previewing your work

To avoid wasting paper and to gain an overall view of how your printed document will look, use **Print Preview** prior to printing.

How to: View in Print Preview

1. Display **Backstage** view, then click on **Print**.
   Print Preview is presented on the right of the window.

2. Note the buttons to move to **Previous Page** or **Next Page** (**1**). You can also type the required page number in the text box and press Enter
3. Note the **Zoom Out** or **Zoom In** buttons (**2**).
4. Note the **Zoom to Page** button in the lower-right corner of the window (**3**), to display a whole page after zooming.

Printing your work

When you are ready to print, you can quickly print the entire active document, or select from a range of print options from the **Print Place**, e.g. print only selected pages, direct to a different printer.

How to: Print using the current settings

1. Display **Backstage** view, then click on **Print**.
   If you are ready to print simply click on the **Print** button, or press Enter.
   You return to where you were originally working. A print message appears briefly on the Status bar.

How to: Select your print options

1. Display **Backstage** view, then click on **Print**.
2. A number of options are presented including:

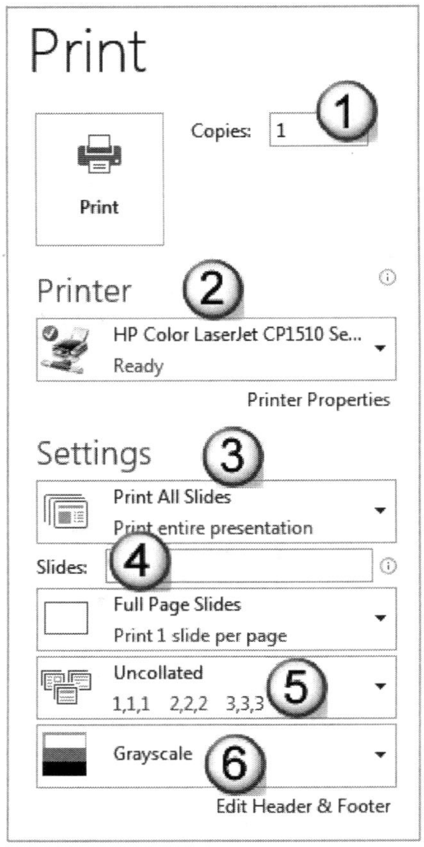

Main printing options

1	**Print: Copies**	Select the number of print copies.
2	**Printer: Name**	Click on the down-arrow to select the required printer.
3	**Settings:**	Choose the slides to print – **Print All Slides**, **Print Selection** (only prints selected slides), **Print Current Slide** (where insertion point is located), **Custom Range**. To print a range of pages, select Custom Range, then enter the page numbers in the **Pages** box, e.g. 3, 5, 8-10.
4	**Slides**	Allows you to choose printing of full page slides or multiple slides per page. This setting also allows you to print your slides with notes or an outline of the slides.
5	**Collated**	When printing multiple copies, **Collated** prints each copy in order, **Uncollated** prints all the copies of page 1 together, then all the copies of page 2, etc.
6	**Colour options**	Allows you to choose to print in color, grayscale or black and white.

Print Ctrl P

Hands-on exercise 16

In this exercise you practise previewing then printing.

- **Open** the presentation *Gardens illustrated.*
- Display the **Backstage** view, click on **Print**.
- Click on the **Options** down-arrow, point to **Grayscale**, then click on **Pure black and white**.
- Click on the **Next Page** button to work through the slides.
- To select the required printer, click on the **Printer** down-arrow, then click on a printer.
- Click on **Print Current Slide**.
- Select the **Grayscale** option.
- Zoom the slide to **120%**.
- Click on **Zoom to Page**
- Click on the **Print** button.
- **Save** your changes.
- **Close** your presentation.

Moving or copying text on a slide

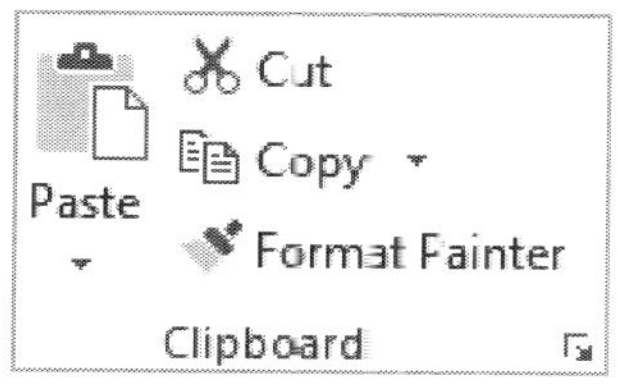

To avoid the need to retype text, PowerPoint allows you to move or copy text to another text placeholder within your presentation. When you **cut** (move) or **copy** text, it is temporarily stored on the Office clipboard until it is **pasted**.

How to: Cut (move) text

1. Select the text to be moved.

2. Display the Home ribbon, then click on the **Cut** button (Clipboard group).

3. Click in a text placeholder where you want to insert the text.
4. Click on the top half of the **Paste** button (Clipboard group).

How to: Copy text

1. Select the text to be copied.

2. Display the Home ribbon, then click on the **Copy** button (Clipboard group).

3. Click in a text placeholder where you want to insert the text.
4. Click on the top half of the **Paste** button (Clipboard group).

As an aside ... *The same text can be pasted again and again until you copy or cut new information to the Clipboard.*

Copy	Ctrl C
Cut	Ctrl X
Paste	Ctrl V

Hands-on exercise 17

In this exercise you practise moving and copying text in a presentation.

- **Open** the presentation *Home security*.

First, you move some text between slides.

- Display slide 3, then select the bullet point:
  Improve your home security
  (You can just drag over the text to select it or click on the bullet point.)
- Click on the **Cut** button.
- Display slide 2.
- Start a new bullet point (beneath the existing) and click on the **Paste** button. Your cut text is relocated.
- On slide 2, select the point:
  Don't leave newspapers outside.
- Click on the **Cut** button.
- Display slide 3.
- Start a new bullet point (beneath the existing) and click on the **Paste** button. Your cut text is relocated.

Next, you copy some text.

- On slide 3, select the following three points (drag over text to select):
  Install window locks
  Install a burglar alarm
  Install door chains
- Click on the **Copy** button.
- Click in the second text placeholder on this slide.
- Click on the **Paste** button. Your text is copied.
- In the second column type the further point:
  Arrange a night security patrol

- Select the point: Don't leave newspapers outside
- Click on the **Copy** button.
- Start a new bullet point (at end of second column).
- Click on the **Paste** button. Your text is copied.
- In the second column select the word 'newspapers'.
  The text is selected.
- Type: bins
  Your new text replaces the existing text.
- **Save** and **close** your presentation.

Terms & concepts review

- How do you display the **Backstage view**?

  ____

  ____

- Describe the two ways to **close** a PowerPoint presentation.

  ____

  ____

- How do you save a presentation that is going to be viewed in PowerPoint 97-2003?

  ____

  ____

  ____

- What colour background is better to use when creating overhead projector slides?

  ____

  ____

- Where do you find Print Preview?

  ____

  ____

Topic 4 – Working with an entire presentation

PowerPoint offers a number of tools to assist you when formatting, re-arranging or modifying your entire presentation.

In this topic you will look at:

- globally modifying slides using a Slide Master
- adding slide footers
- re-arranging slides in Slide Sorter view and the Slide tab
- modifying slide text using the Outline tab in the navigation pane.

Using the Slide Master

Until now you have been editing directly on a slide and changing only that slide, e.g. changing a font size or bullets. However, PowerPoint provides a **Slide Master** to help you make global changes. The Slide Master provides a separate master for each layout, e.g. Title Slide Layout, Title and Content Layout, Section Header Layout. Each layout indicates how many slides in the presentation use that layout.

If you want a graphic or a piece of text to appear on all slides, add it to the Slide Master (first thumbnail). If you want the item to appear only on a specific layout, then add it to the relevant layout master instead.

> ***For example** … If you want a graphic to appear on the title slide only, add the graphic to the Title Slide Layout. If you want a graphic to appear on slides with a title and content only, add the graphic to the Title and Content Layout.*

Use the Slide Master to ensure a consistent company image (e.g. a logo size and placement), and consistent formatting is maintained throughout a presentation.

How to: Display the Slide Master

1. Display the View ribbon, then click on the **Slide Master** button (Master Views group). Slide Master View is presented. A Slide Master tab is added to the ribbon and various thumbnails appear in the left pane. Point to each thumbnail to display a ScreenTip showing the name of the layout.
2. The first thumbnail in the left pane is the Slide Master. The thumbnails below are for each of the layouts.

3. Click on the required master/layout.
4. To exit the Slide Master, click on the **Close Master View** button (Slide Master ribbon).

How to: Change the colour scheme or font throughout your presentation

1. Display the **Slide Master.**
2. Click on the **Colors or Fonts** down-arrow (Slide Master ribbon, Background group), point to a font theme for a live preview. Click on the required theme.

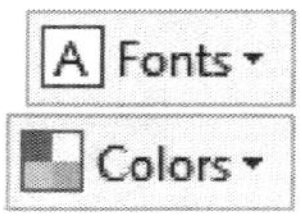

3. To exit the Slide Master, click on the **Close Master View** button, or display Normal view (Status bar icon).

Hands-on exercise 18

In this exercise you practise making changes to the Slide Master.

- **Open** the presentation *Gardens illustrated.*
- Display the View ribbon, then click on the **Slide Master** button (Presentation group). Slide Master View is presented.
  A Slide Master tab is added to the ribbon and various thumbnails appear in the left pane.
  Point to each thumbnail to display a ScreenTip showing the name of the layout.
- Click on the Title and Content Layout thumbnail.
- Click in the title placeholder.
- Click on the **Fonts** button (Background group), point to the **Century Gothic** theme, note the preview, then click on the theme.
- Select the first line of text in the content placeholder (first level text).

- Display the Home ribbon, then click on the **Increase Font Size** button (Font group).
- Return to Slide Master view ribbon.
- Click on the Title Slide Layout thumbnail.
- Select the text in the top title placeholder.
- Display the Home ribbon, then click on the **Font Color** down-arrow (Font group). Select black for the title.
- **Close Master View.**
- Scroll through your slides and observe the changes.
- **Save** your changes.

Adding a slide footer

A **slide footer** is commonly used to display information such as the date of your presentation and the slide or page number.

How to: Add a slide footer

1. Display your presentation in Normal view.
2. Display the Insert ribbon, then click on the **Header and Footer** button (Text group). The Header and Footer dialogue box is presented.

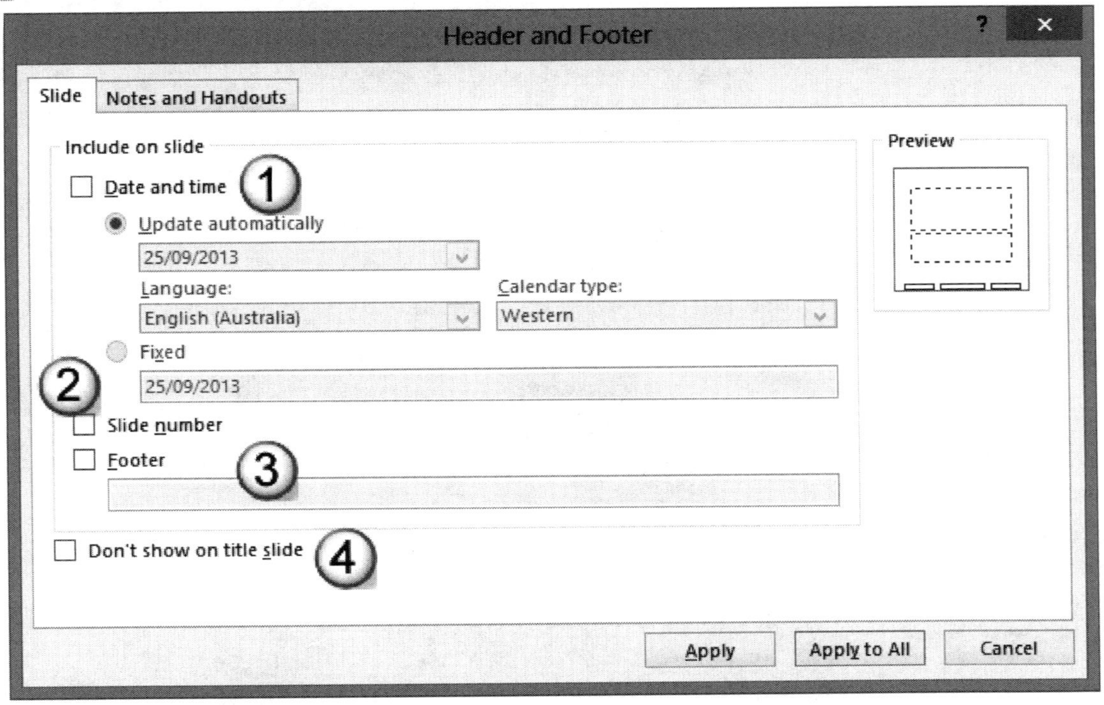

3. Ensure the Slide tab is selected.
4. Select the required option:

1	**Date and time**	If you require a date, ensure this option is selected, then click on **Update automatically** for PowerPoint to set the current date. Or, click on **Fixed** and type a date (or other text, e.g. version number). The date appears on the left of the slide.

(2)	**Slide number**	Select this option if you require your slides to be numbered. The number appears on the right of the slide. (Avoid using – can be distracting.)
(3)	**Footer**	Select then type additional footer text if required.
(4)	**Don't show on title slide**	Select this option if you only want to apply the changes to the body of the presentation.

5. Ensure the **Language** is English (Australian).
6. Click on **Apply** to change an individual slide
   ~or~
   Click on **Apply to All**.

Hands-on exercise 19

In this exercise you practise adding a footer to your presentation.

- Using the presentation *Gardens illustrated*, display your presentation in Normal view.
- Display the Insert ribbon, then click on the **Header and Footer** button (Text group). The Header and Footer dialogue box is presented.
- Select the **Date and time** option. Ensure **Update Automatically** is highlighted and the **Language** is English (Australian).
- Click in the **Footer** option and type the text:
  In Your Garden Magazine Launch
- Select the **Don't show on title slide** option.
- Click on **Apply to All**.
- Run the Slide Show from slide 1, observing your footer.
- **Save** your changes.
- **Close** your presentation.

Hints & tips

You can change the position of your footer in the Slide Master. Drag the placeholder to the new position.

Re-arranging your slides

To easily move, copy or delete slides, view your presentation in Slide Sorter view or use the Slides tab in the navigation pane. In both views you can see slide thumbnails. This makes it easy to select a slide, and then move, copy or delete it.

How to: Re-arrange slides in Slide Sorter view

1. View your presentation in **Slide Sorter** view.
2. If necessary, click on the **Zoom Out** button to reduce the magnification so that you can see more slides.

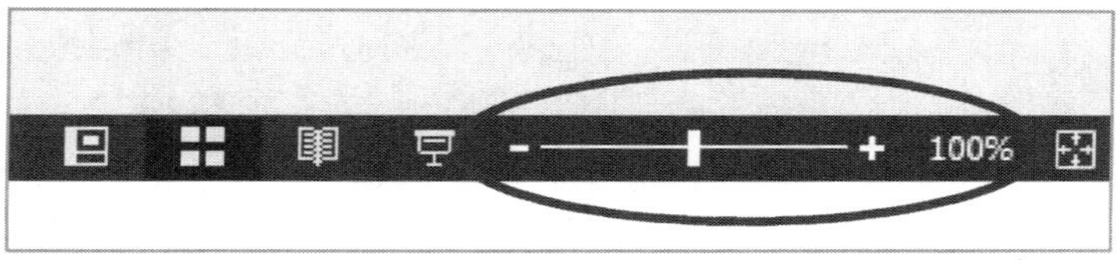

3. To **delete** a slide, click on the slide, then press Delete. To **move** a slide, point to the slide, then drag it to a new position beside another slide (note the line appearing between the slides to indicate a new location). To **copy** a slide, press and hold Ctrl as you drag a slide to a new location.
4. To return to Normal view, double-click on a slide *~or~*
   Click on the **Normal** view button (Status bar).

How to: Re-arrange slides using the Navigation Pane

1. Display your presentation in Normal view.
2. To **delete** a slide, click on the slide, then press Delete.
   To **move** a slide, point to the slide, then drag it to a new position beside another slide (note the line appearing between the slides to indicate a new location). To **copy** a slide, press and hold Ctrl as you drag a slide to a new location.

***As an aside** … Note also the **Delete** button on the Home ribbon.*

Hands-on exercise 20

In this exercise you practise editing a slide presentation in Slide Sorter view.

- **Open** the presentation *Wave boards.*
- Scroll through this seven-slide presentation. Some of the slides appear to be in the wrong order.
- View your presentation in **Slide Sorter** view.

First, you move the slides into the correct position.

- Click on the last slide: **Launching your board**, then drag and release it after the second slide: **What you will learn**
  (note the line appearing between the slides to indicate a new location.)
- Using this method, rearrange the slides into the following order:
  1. Sailing a wave board
  2. What you will learn
  3. Launching your board
  4. Turning your board
  5. Returning to shore
  6. The next session
  7. Congratulations

At the last minute, the next session is cancelled.

- Ensure the sixth slide is selected: **The next session**, then press Delete.

Next, you decide to add a slide that will help the students review the skills they have gained during the course. To save time, you copy an existing slide and edit it.

- In Slide Sorter view, click on the third slide: **Launching your board**.
- Press Ctrl and drag this slide in front of the last slide: **Congratulations**
- Double-click on the copied slide (slide 6) to display in **Normal** view.
- Change the title of the slide to: What you have mastered
- Click on the first slide in the Navigation Pane.
- Run your **Reading View**.
- **Save** your changes.
- **Close** your presentation.

Hands-on exercise 21

In this exercise you continue to practice moving slides.

- Open you presentation *Market Brainstorming*.
- Review the presentation in **Reading View**. Take note of the Agenda slide.
- What is the order of the meeting on the agenda slide?

  ____
  ____
  ____
  ____
  ____
  ____

- Rearrange the slides after the Agenda slide in either **Slide View** or the **Navigation Pane** to reflect the points on the Agenda slide.
- **Save** and **close** your presentation.

Working in the Outline View

When you are working with a large presentation, it is important that the text flow is correct. By working in the outline view you can concentrate on text content and flow without being distracted by the colour, pictures or formatting of slides.

You can type your entire presentation in the outline view. You can easily demote text on a slide to a lower level, promote text to a higher level or move points up or down.

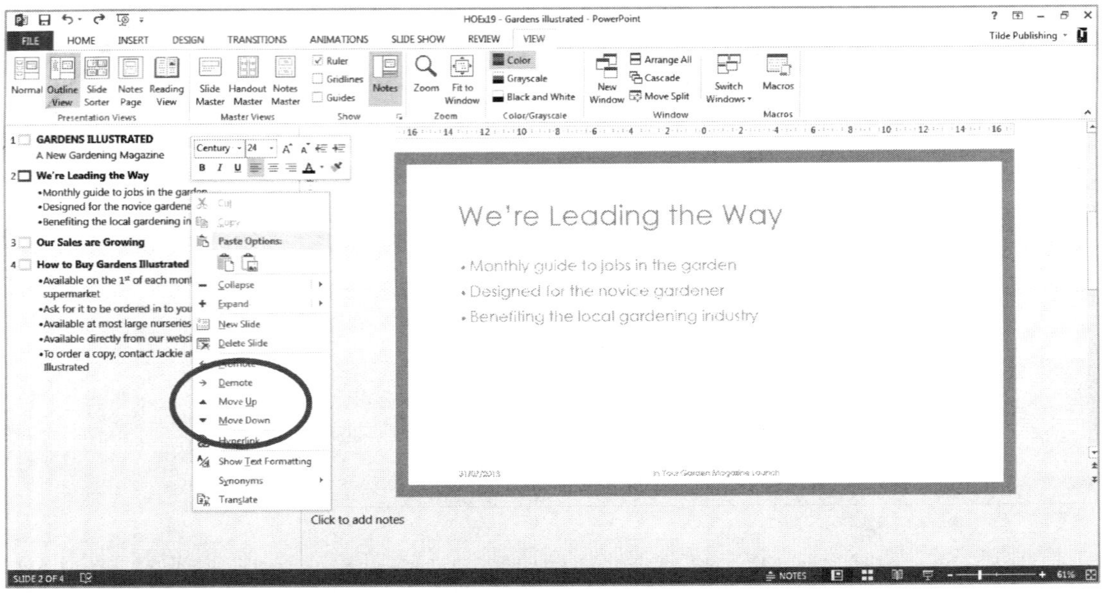

The outline of a presentation

How to: Display the slide outline

1. Display the View ribbon, then click on the **Outline View** button. (Presentation views group).

As an aside *... To zoom the size of the text on the Outline tab, click in the text, display the View ribbon, then click on the* ***Zoom*** *button.*

How to: Work in a presentation outline

1. Press Tab in the Outline pane to demote text.
2. Press Shift Tab in the Outline pane to promote text.
   When you promote text to the highest level it becomes a new slide.

~or~

1. Right-click on the Outline pane, then click on the required option from the shortcut menu.

Promote		Click on a point, then click on the **Promote** button to increase its level of importance.
Demote		Click on a point or title, then click on the **Demote** button to lower its level of importance.
Move Up		Click on a point or title, then click on the **Move Up** button to move text up the presentation.
Move Down		Click on a point or title, then click on the **Move Down** button to move text down the presentation.
Collapse		Click on a slide title, then click on the **Collapse** button to collapse (hide) the slide text.
Collapse All		Click on to display slide titles only (Click on Collapse arrow to show Collapse All).

Expand	+	Click on a slide title, then click on the **Expand** button to display collapsed slide text.
Expand All		Click on to display the entire presentation. (Use after the slides have been collapsed) (Click on Collapse arrow to show Collapse All).
Show Formatting		Click on to switch between displaying text formatting and plain text.

How to: Print your outline

1. Display **Backstage** view, then click on **Print**.
   The Print screen is presented.
2. Click on **Full Page Slides** down-arrow, then click on **Outline**.

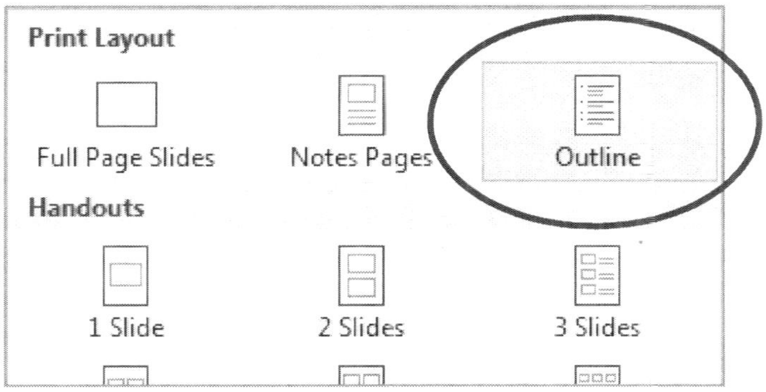

3. Click on **OK**.

Hands-on exercise 22

In this exercise you create a presentation using the Outline View.

- Create a **new** blank presentation.
- Display the View ribbon, then click on the **Outline View** button.
- Click next to the first slide icon presented in the Outline Pane.
- Type the slide title: Painting with Stains
- Press Enter
- To demote the next point, press Tab
- Type: Advice from your hardware store
- Press Enter

  (Also note your slide developing.)
- To promote the next point, press Shift Tab
- Type the slide title: Getting Good Results
- Press Enter
- To demote the next point, press Tab
- Type: Get to know your timber

- Press Enter
- Type: Always stir the stain before you begin
- Press Enter
- To promote the next point, press Shift Tab
- Type the slide title: Timber Characteristics
- Press Enter
- Press Tab
- Type the following, pressing Enter after each line:

  Treated Pine
  Make sure the treatment is dry before you stain
  Oregon
  Has a high resin content
  Western Red Cedar
  A soft timber which takes stain easily

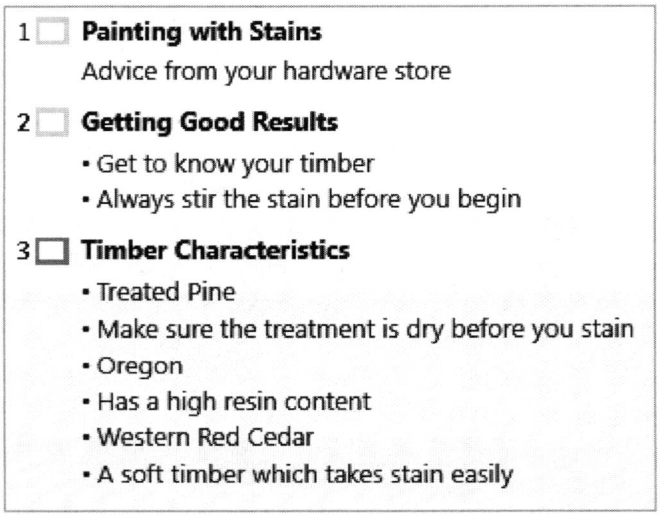

- You now have a 3-slide presentation.
- Check your spelling.
- **Save** your presentation as *Painting*.
- Display your presentation in **normal** view.
- Apply a theme of your choice.
- Display the first slide and scroll through your presentation.
- Go back to **outline view**.

Next, you rearrange some of your text.

- In the Outline pane under the slide title **Timber Characteristics**, right-click on the text: Make sure the treatment...
- Click on the **Demote** button.
- Right-click on the text: Has a high resin ... then click on the **Demote** button.

- Right-click on the text: A soft timber ...
  then click on the **Demote** button.
- Point to the **Oregon** bullet symbol (your mouse pointer becomes a four-way arrow), then click.
  This selects the Oregon point and it's sub-text.
- Right-click on the selected text, then click on the **Move Up** button
  Repeat to move the text to the top of the slide.
- Point to the **Treated Pine** bullet symbol (your mouse pointer becomes a four-way arrow), then click.
- Right-click on the selected text, then click on the **Move Down** button.
  Repeat to move the text to the bottom of the slide.
- Right-click on the outline text, point to **Collapse**, then click on **Collapse All**.
  Observe the text has collapsed (become hidden) beneath the slide titles.
- Right-click on the slide title: **Timber Characteristics**
- Click on the **Move Up** button to move this slide above: **Getting Good Results**
- Right-click on the outline text, point to **Expand**, then click on **Expand All**.
  Observe all the text has expanded beneath the slide titles and the entire **Timber Characteristics** slide and its sub-text have been relocated

Finally, you print preview then print your slide.

- Display **Backstage** view, click on **Print**.
- Use the **Next Page/Previous Page** buttons to move through your slides.
- Click on the **Full Page Slides** down-arrow, then click on **Outline**.
- Click on the **Print** button.
- Return to **normal view.**
- **Save** your changes.
- **Close** your presentation.

Consolidation task 1

In this task you create a presentation using the outline pane.

- Create a **new** blank presentation.
- Size your slides for: **On-screen Show (16:10)**.
- Create the following in the outline pane.

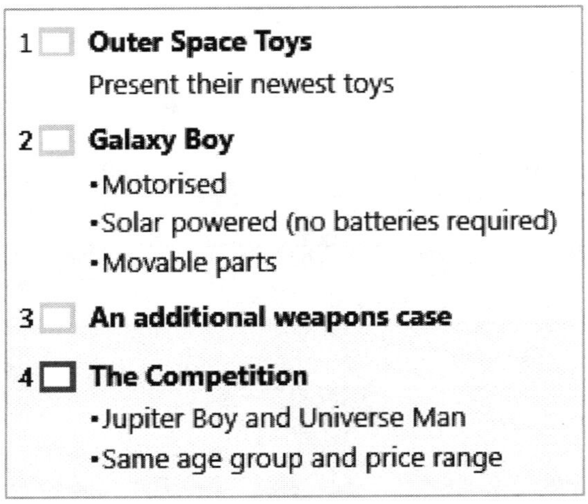

- **Save** your presentation as *Outer space*.
- Check your spelling.
- Move the bullet point: Movable parts above the bullet point: Motorised
- Demote the bullet point: An additional weapons case
- Apply the theme **Depth**.
- Insert a footer on all slides (except the title slide) which shows the current date and footer text of: Outer Space Toys Pty Ltd.
- **Save** your changes.
- **Close** your presentation.

Topic 5 – Pictures, placeholders, shapes & tables

Using pictures and shapes on a slide not only makes it more attractive and interesting, but it can also help your audience gain an immediate impression of what a slide is about.

Inserting picture files

You can easily insert an online picture onto a slide using a placeholder. You can also add a picture without using a placeholder, for a more freeform layout.

How to: Insert an online picture

1. Add a slide with a slide layout that includes …**Content**.

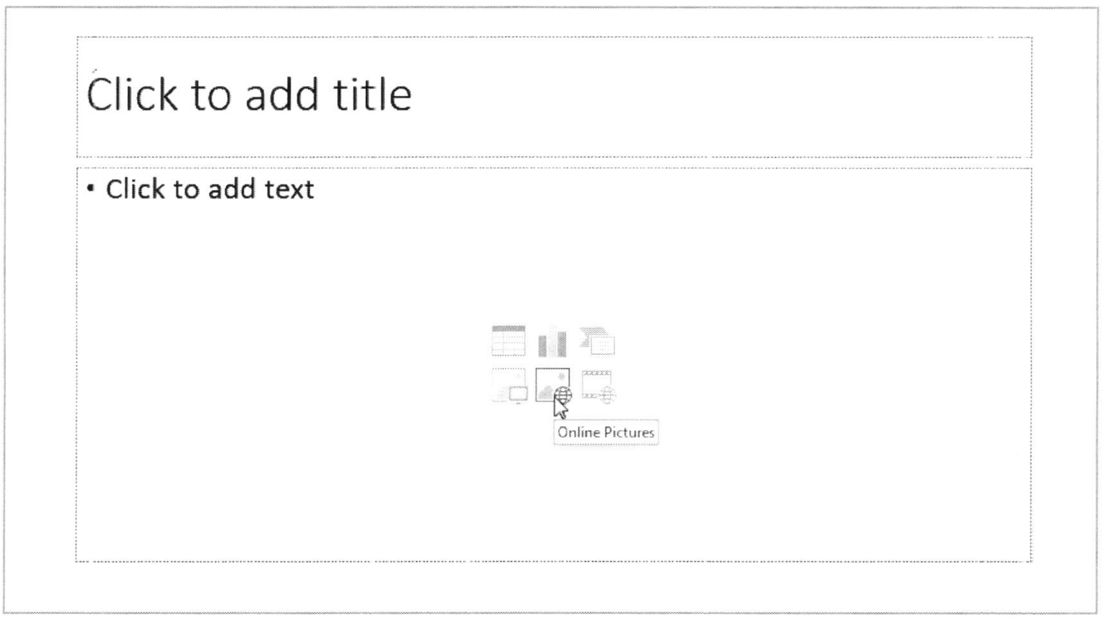

2. Click on the **Online Pictures** icon in the placeholder.

The Insert Pictures dialogue box is presented.

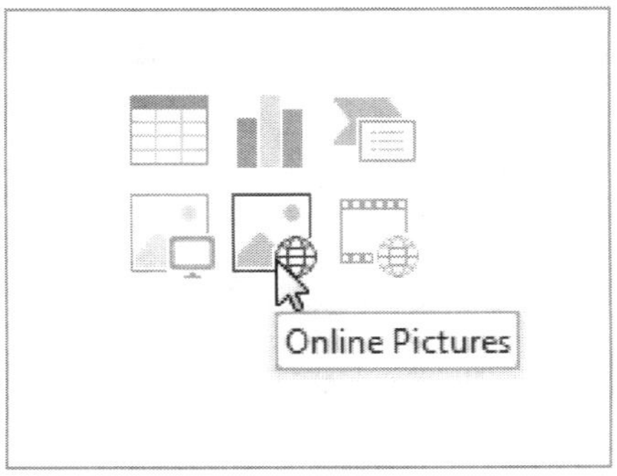

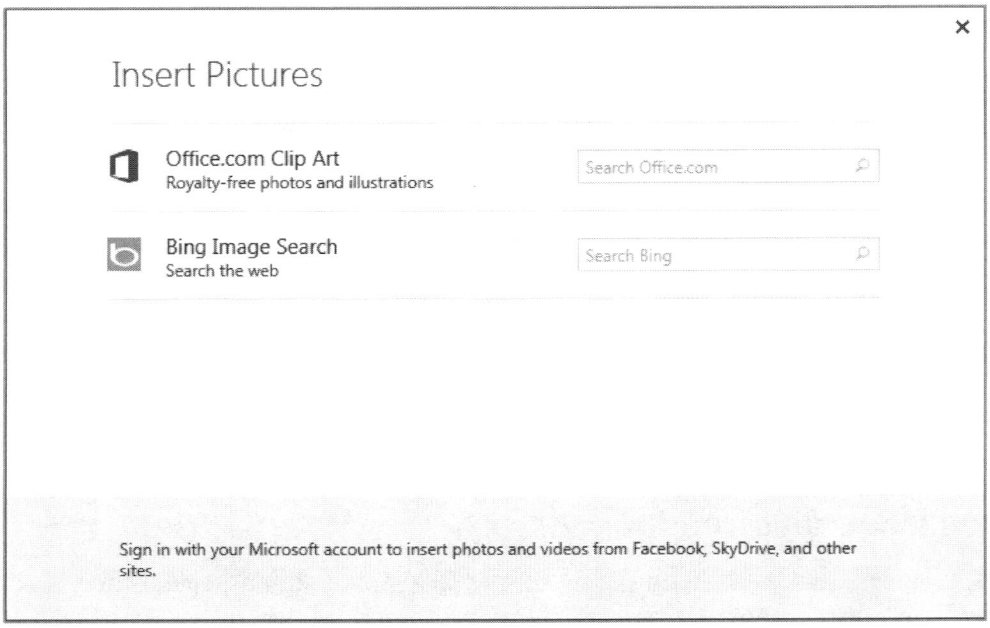

3. In the search box for **Office.com Clip Art** type a word or phrase that best describes the picture you want in the **Search for** text box.

4. Press Enter or click on the magnifying glass.
   A number of pictures are displayed.

5. Click on the required Clip Art picture, then click on **Insert.**
   The picture is inserted into your placeholder.
   Note the **Picture Tools** added on a new **Format** Ribbon. This is displayed while the picture is selected.

How to: Insert a picture file with a placeholder

1. Add a slide with a slide layout that includes …**Content**.
2. Click on the **Insert Picture from File** icon in the placeholder.
   The Insert Picture dialogue box is presented.

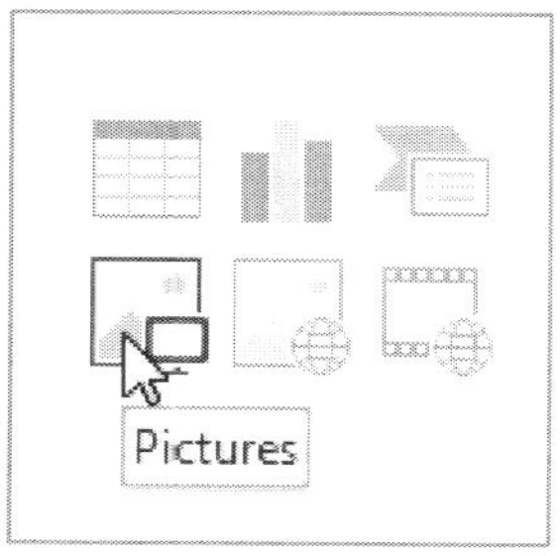

3. Locate and select your picture file.
4. Click on **Insert**.
   The selected picture is inserted into the placeholder.

How to: Insert a online picture or picture file without a placeholder

1. Display the Insert ribbon, then click on the **Pictures** or **Online Pictures** buttons (Images group).
2. Follow steps as previously. Pictures are inserted freely on the slide.

Hands-on exercise 23

In this exercise you improve the look of a slide by incorporating an online picture.

- **Open** the presentation *Home security*.
- Display slide 2.
- Click on the **Online Pictures** icon in the placeholder.

  The Insert dialogue box is presented.
- In the **Search Office.com** search box, type: security
- Press Enter.
- Click on a relevant picture of your choice, then click on **Insert.**
  The picture is inserted into your placeholder.
  Note the Picture Tools added on a new Format Ribbon.
  This is displayed while the picture is selected.
- View your **Slide Master**, then select the first Slide Master thumbnail on the left which applies to all slides.

- Display the Insert ribbon, then click on the **Pictures** button (Images group). Locate and insert the supplied picture file from your exercise files folder: *Key logo*.
- Drag the 'logo' to the bottom left of the master.
- Display the slides in **Normal view**. Scroll through the slides.
- **Save** your changes.

> ***As an aside*** *... Use one large picture on a slide rather than numerous small pictures. Too many pictures can make a slide look busy and confusing.*

Manipulating your pictures

You can easily resize and move a picture once it has been inserted.

How to: Resize a picture

1. Sizing handles appear around a picture when it is selected. (Double-click on a picture if it is not selected.)

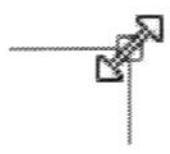

2. Point to a sizing handle. Your mouse pointer becomes a two-way arrow. To ensure you size the picture proportionately, point to one of the corner handles.
3. Drag the sizing handle to a new size.

> ***As an aside*** *... If you drag the sizing handles from the side, you will find your picture will distort. To stop the distortion, always drag from the corners.*

How to: Rotate a picture

You can rotate a picture to any angle or simply flip it to face the other way.

1. Double click on the picture (to display the Picture Tools/Format ribbon).
2. Click on the **Rotate** button, then select from the required option.

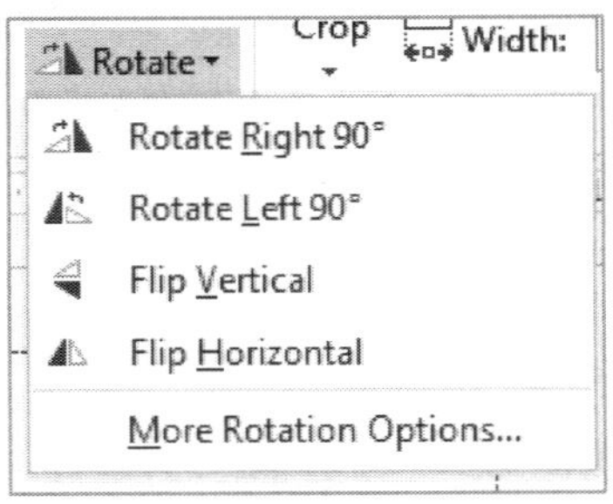

~or~

1. Select the picture, then click on the circular arrow rotation handle at the top of the picture and move the mouse left or right to change the direction.

> ***As an aside*** *... To remove the rotation, click on* ***Rotate, More Rotation Options****, then on the Size tab, set the rotation to 0.*

How to: Move a picture

1. Point to your picture. A four-way arrow is attached to your mouse pointer. Drag your picture to a new position on a slide.

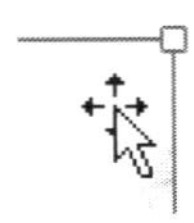

***As an aside** … To delete a picture ensure it is selected then press* Delete.

How to: Recolour a picture

1. Double-click on a picture to display the Picture Tools/Format ribbon.
2. Click on the **Color** button (Adjust group).

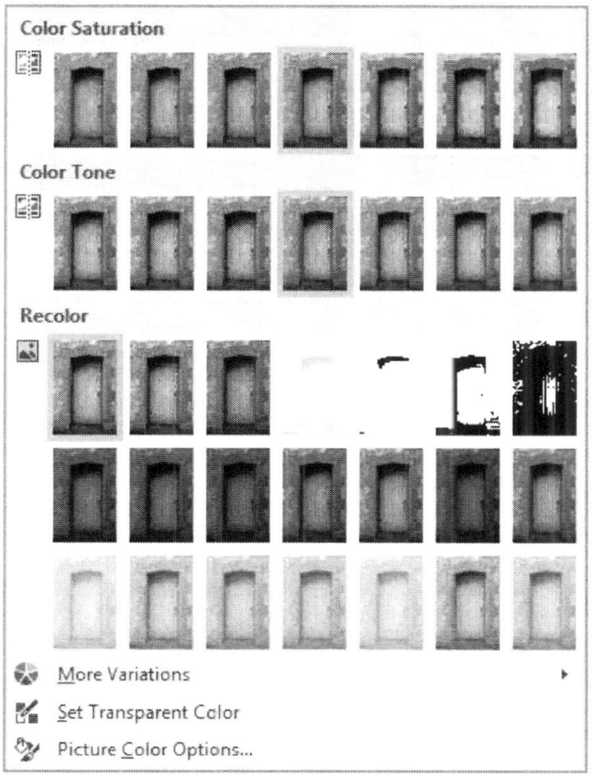

3. Click on one of the colour variations (note the live preview).

How to: Crop (trim) a picture

1. Double-click on a picture to display the Picture Tools/Format ribbon.
2. Click on the top half of the **Crop** button (Size group).
3. Drag on one of the sizing handles that surround the picture.

4. Click back on the **Crop** button to finish or press Esc.

***As an aside** … Even though a picture has been cropped, at any time you can turn the crop tool back on, drag out on a cropping handle and re-display the portion of the picture you previously cropped.*

Hands-on exercise 24

In this exercise you practise resizing and moving a picture.

- Using the presentation *Home security*, display slide 2, then double-click on your picture to select it and display the Picture Tools/Format ribbon.
- Point to a corner-sizing handle.
  Your mouse pointer becomes a two-way arrow.
- Drag the sizing handle so that your picture is of appropriate size.
- Position the mouse pointer on the circular arrow rotation handle. Your mouse pointer becomes a circular arrow.
- Drag to rotate.
- Point to the picture. A four-way arrow is attached to your mouse pointer.
- Drag the picture to the bottom-right corner of the slide.
- Keeping the picture selected, click on the **Colour** button (Adjust group) and experiment on different colours.
- Click on the top half of the **Crop** button (Size group) and experiment. **Undo** any changes you are not happy with.
- **Save** your changes.
- **Close** your presentation.

***As an aside** ... Note also the **Height** and **Width** measurements for a picture on the Format ribbon, Size group.*

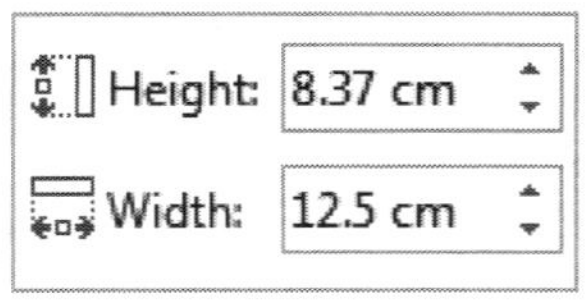

How to: Crop to a shape

1. Double-click on a picture to select it (and display Picture Tools/Format ribbon).
2. Click on the bottom half of the **Crop** button (Size group).
3. Point to **Crop to Shape**, then click on a shape.

Working with placeholders

When text or an object has been inserted in a **placeholder**, the placeholder can be resized or relocated. You do not need to work with the size or placement established by the slide layout.

How to: Move a placeholder

1. Click on the placeholder to select.
2. Position your mouse pointer over the border of the placeholder until your pointer becomes a four-way arrow.
3. Drag the placeholder box to the new position.

How to: Change the size of a placeholder

1. Click on the placeholder to select.
2. Point to a sizing handle on the border of the placeholder. Your mouse pointer becomes a two-way arrow.
3. Drag to a new size.

> ***As an aside*** *...Note the **Reset** button on the Home ribbon to reset the position and size (and formatting) of placeholders.*

How to: Delete a placeholder

1. Click on the placeholder to select.
2. Click on the border of the placeholder then press Delete.

Hands-on exercise 25

In this exercise you practise moving and sizing placeholders.

- **Open** the presentation *Gardens illustrated.*
- On slide 1, click on the title placeholder to select.
- With the placeholder selected, position your mouse pointer over the left border.
- Drag your mouse right so the placeholder is in line with the white line.
- Select the right border sizing handle of the placeholder and drag left to line up with the white line.
- View the **Slide Master**. Select the **Title and Content Layout**.
- Insert the supplied picture file *Tree* (no placeholder). Position in the bottom-right corner of the layout.
- Display the slides in Normal view. Scroll through the slides.
- **Save** your changes.
- **Close** your presentation.

Inserting basic shapes

PowerPoint provides an extensive range of preconfigured shapes that you can insert into your slides. These include basic shapes, lines and arrows, flowchart symbols and callouts.

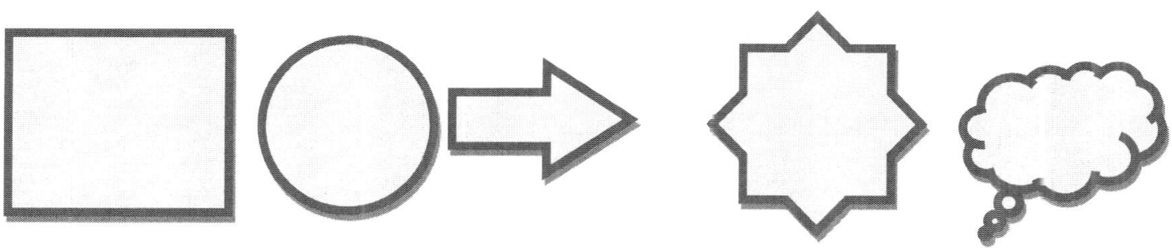

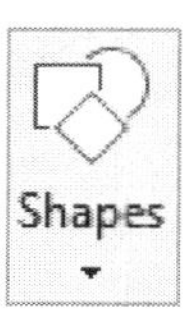

How to: Draw a shape

1. Display the Insert ribbon, then click on the **Shapes** button (Illustrations group). The Shapes gallery is presented.

2. Click on the shape you want to insert.
   Your mouse pointer becomes a cross.
3. Drag diagonally to create your shape.
   Note the Drawing Tools added on a new Format Ribbon.
   - To **resize** a shape, select and drag on a sizing handle at the end or corner.
   - To **move** a shape, point to it and drag.
   - To **copy** a shape, press Ctrl and drag.
   - To **delete** a shape, select and press Delete.
   - To **rotate** a shape, select and drag the green rotate handle.

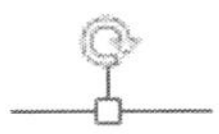

How to: Change a shape fill colour

1. Double-click on the shape to display the Drawing Tools/Format ribbon.

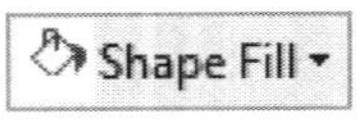

2. Click on the **Shape Fill** down-arrow (Shape Styles group), then click on the required colour.

How to: Change a shape outline

1. Double-click on the shape to display the Drawing Tools/Format ribbon.
2. Click on the **Shape Outline** down-arrow (Shape Styles group), then click on the required colour.

How to: Change a shape effect

1. Double-click on the shape to display the Drawing Tools/Format ribbon.

2. Click on the **Shape Effect** down-arrow (Shape Styles group), point to the required effect, then click on the required option.

How to: Add text to a shape

1. Click on the shape and start typing.

Hints & tips

What if I want to draw a square or a circle?

Press Shift as you draw with a Rectangle shape to draw a square.

Press Shift as you draw with the Oval shape to draw a circle.

What if I cannot keep my lines straight as I draw?

Press Shift as you draw a line to keep it straight.

What if I see an additional yellow sizing handle on an object?

Some of the shapes have an additional yellow adjust handle. Point to the handle and drag to change the depth or angle.

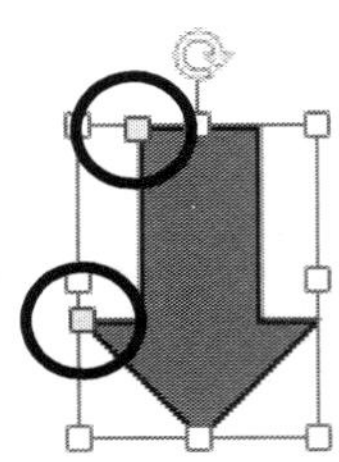

What if I want to move multiple objects together?

Select the objects you want to keep together (holding the [Shift] key down while you click on them), then click on **Group** down arrow (Arrange group) then select **Group**. You can now move or resize all of the objects together.

How can I align two shapes?

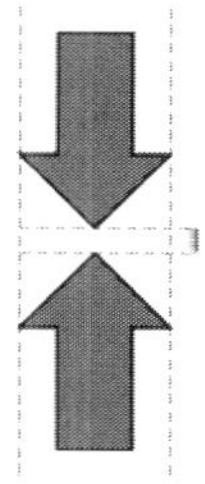

PowerPoint shows dotted lines around objects when you are aligning two or more objects.

~or~

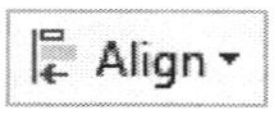

Click on the first shape, press [Shift] and click on the second shape (to select both shapes). Click on the **Align** button (Drawing Tools/Format ribbon, Arrange group), then click on the required alignment, e.g. Align Top.

Hands-on exercise 26

In this exercise you practise creating a house out of shapes.

- **Open** the presentation *Home security*.
- Insert a new slide (layout: blank).
- Insert a square (remember to hold the [Shift] key down).
- Above the square, insert a triangle (for the roof).
- Select both shapes, click on **Align**, then **Align Centre** (Arrange group).
- To create the door, draw a rectangle.
- Change the **Shape Fill** (Shape Styles group) colour of the rectangle.
- Select the rectangle and square, then **Align Center**.
- Insert 1 square for a window.
- Change the **Shape Fill** colour of the square (window).
- Click on the square (window), hold down the [Ctrl] key to copy the square.
- Position and align the windows appropriately (Align middle).
- Change any **Shape Fill** or **Shape Outline** as appropriate.
- Select all of the shapes (press [Ctrl] [A]).
- Experiment with **Shape Effects**. Choose an effect of your choice.
- While all of the shapes are still selected, group them by clicking on the **Group** down arrow, then select Group (arrange)
- **Save** and **close** your presentation.

Inserting a table

You can create a **table** on a slide quickly and easily in PowerPoint.

How to: Insert a table with a placeholder

1. Add a slide with a slide layout that includes ...**Content**.
2. Click on the **Insert Table** icon in the placeholder. The Insert Table dialogue box is presented.

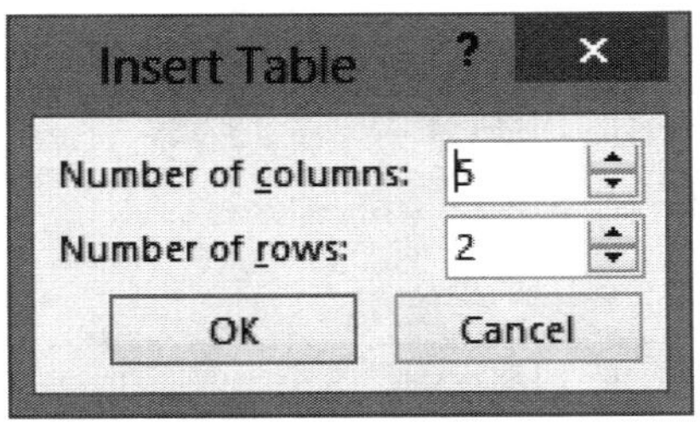

3. Select the required number of columns and rows.
4. Click on **OK**.
   The table is inserted into the placeholder with a default format. Two new ribbons are displayed with Table Tools (Design and Layout). The Design ribbon is active.

How to: Insert a table without a placeholder

1. Display the Insert ribbon, then click on the **Table** button (Table group). A drop-down box appears.

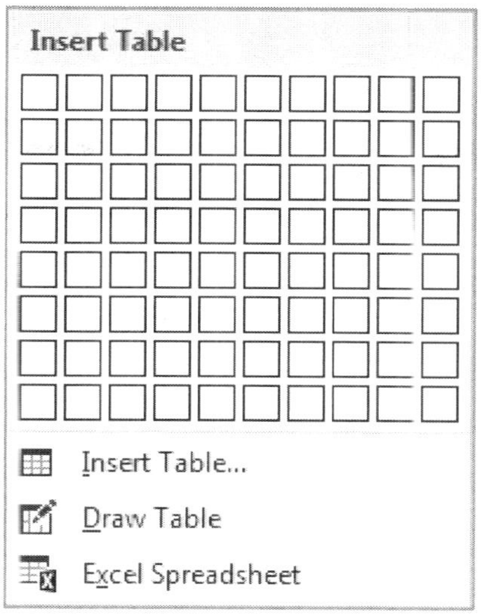

2. Drag over the cells in the grid to indicate the number of rows and columns required. A table is inserted on the slide.

How to: Enter data

1. Your insertion point is flashing in the first cell, type the required data.
2. Press [Tab] to move to the next cell. (If you press [Enter] you will simply get a new line within the same cell.)
3. If you press [Tab] from the end of the final cell in a table, a new row is added.

How to: Move within a table - mouse method

1. Point to the new location and click.

How to: Move within a table - keyboard methods

Next cell	[Tab] or [→]
Previous cell	[Shift] [Tab] or [←]
Next row	[↓]
Previous row	[↑]

How to: Select within a table - mouse methods

Row	Position the mouse pointer outside the table, beside a row. The mouse pointer becomes a black arrow. Click once or drag down to select multiple rows.	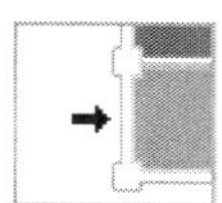
Column	Position the mouse pointer at the top of a column until a black down-arrow is displayed, then click or drag across to select multiple columns.	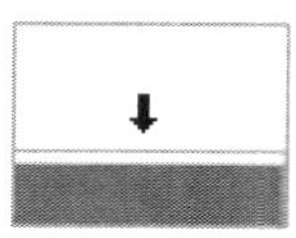
Cell	Position the mouse pointer in the cell to the left of the text. The mouse pointer becomes a black arrow. Click to select the cell.	

How to: Insert/delete a row/column

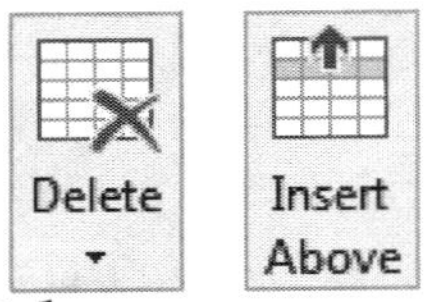

1. Select a row or column.
2. Display the Table Tools/Layout ribbon.
3. Click on the required button in the **Rows & Columns** group.

How to: Change column width

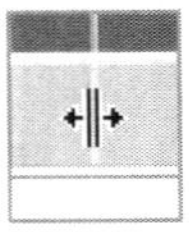

1. Position the mouse pointer on the required gridline.
   The mouse pointer becomes a double-headed arrow.
2. Drag the gridline to a new position.

***As an aside** … Text in a table does not appear in Outline.*

How to: Move a table

1. Point to a border of the table.
   The mouse pointer becomes a four-way arrow.
2. Drag to a new location.

How to: Resize a table

1. Point to a corner or side resize handle.
   The mouse pointer becomes a two-way arrow.
2. Drag in/out.

***As an aside** … To resize proportionately, drag on a corner sizing handle. Hold* Shift *as you drag to also adjust font size.*

Hands-on exercise 27

In this exercise you practise creating a table.

- Create a **new** blank presentation.
- Change the layout to **Title and Content**.
- Click in the title placeholder, then type: Table Sample
- Click on the **Insert Table** icon in the placeholder.
  The Insert Table dialogue box is presented.
- Select 5 columns and 7 rows.
- Click on **OK**.
  The table is inserted into the placeholder with a default format. Two new ribbons are displayed with Table Tools (Design and Layout). The Design ribbon is active.
- Enter the following data:

Monday	Tuesday	Wednesday	Thursday	Friday
100	235	700	690	590

- Practice moving and selecting in the table.
- Delete the bottom 2 rows.

- Drag on the gridline to the right of Monday to reduce the column size.

- Using the resize handle in the bottom-right corner of the table, reduce the size of the table.
- Click and drag the table to the centre of the slide.
- **Save** your slide as *Table example*.

Applying table styles, borders and shading

You can apply other pre-designed table **styles** and manually adjust borders and shading.

How to: Apply table styles

1. Click in the table.
2. Display the Design ribbon, point to any option in the **Tables Styles** group to see the design effect previewed on your table. Click on the **More** arrow to display the full gallery of styles.
3. Click on the required style to apply. The first option on the ribbon is plain.

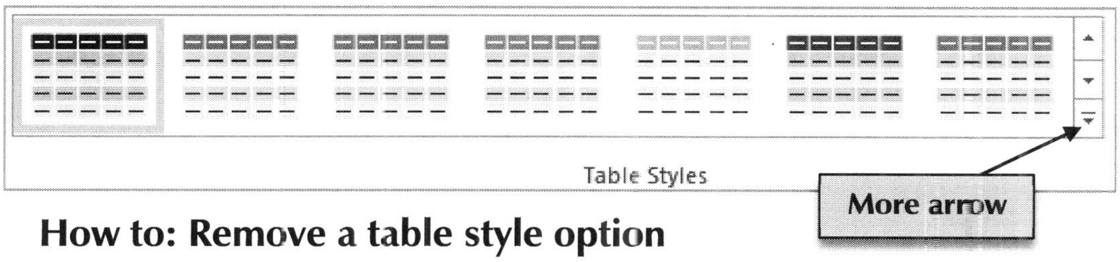

How to: Remove a table style option

1. Click in the table.
2. Display the Design ribbon, click to remove a selected option in the **Table Style Options** group, e.g. to remove formatting on the first (header) row.

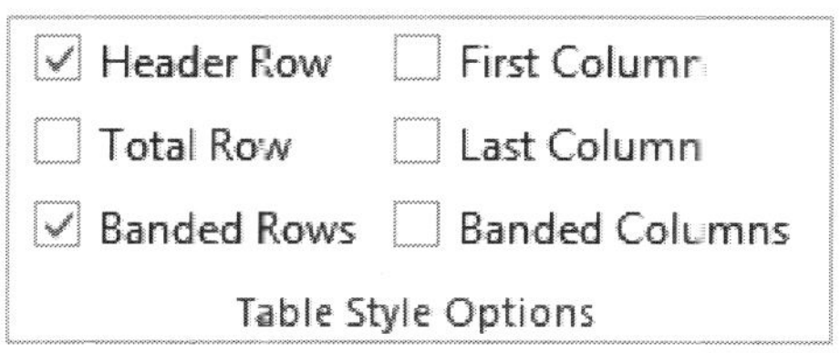

How to: Adjust table shading

1. Select the required cell, row or column.
2. Display the Design ribbon, click on the **Shading** button (Table Styles group). A gallery of colours is presented organised by themes. Point to a colour selection to see the design effect previewed on your table.
3. Click on a shading of your choice.

As an aside … To remove shading from a table, select the cells, click on the ***Shading*** *button, then click on* ***No Fill.***

How to: Adjust table borders

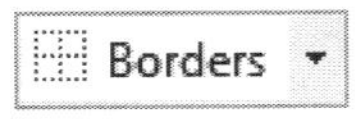

1. Select the required cell, row or column.
2. Display the Design ribbon, click on the **Borders** down-arrow (Table Styles group). A list of options is presented.
3. Click on the required border option.

As an aside …Note that the last border selected is stored behind the button (note picture on button) so if you click directly on the button instead of the down-arrow the currently selected option is applied immediately.

Hands-on exercise 28

In this exercise you practise creating a table.

- Using the presentation *Table example*, click in the table to select.
- In the **Table Style Options**, click on the option **Header Row**. Note the effect. Click again on **Header Row**.
- Display the Design ribbon and place your mouse over different themes. Notice how the table changes in the different themes.
- Apply a theme of your choice.
- Display the Table Tools/Design ribbon, point to any option in the **Tables Styles** group to see the design effect previewed on your table. Click on the **More** arrow, then click on the style **Light Style 1**.
- Select the first row.
- Display the Home ribbon and click on the centre alignment button (Paragraph group).
- Select all the remaining rows and apply right.
- Display the Table Tools/Design ribbon and select all the columns.
- Click on the **Borders** down-arrow, then click on **All Borders**.
- **Save** your changes.
- **Close** your presentation.

Consolidation task 2

In this task you create an overhead slide to publicise an event.

- Create a new **blank** presentation.
- Change the page setup to **overhead**.
- Change the slide layout to **Two Content**.
- Type the text below in the first and second text columns.

Craft workshops	Toy City 5th May
Fashion parades	Fun Run 10th May
Painting classes	Kid's Day 20th May
Upholstery	Final party with fireworks 30th May
Book now!	

- Check your spelling.
- Apply a suitable theme.
- Delete the title placeholder.
- Using the shapes, create the following in place of the title. If necessary, resize and move the text placeholders to allow room for your design.
- Select appropriate colours/effects/borders for you title.

- Insert an online picture and recolour to match the theme.
- **Save** your slide as *May events.*
- **Preview** your presentation. Make any necessary changes.
- **Close** your presentation.

Just an example of the finished presentation. Yours may look slightly different.

Topic 6 – Creating a chart

Charts are a very effective way of presenting numerical data required in a presentation.

Charting with PowerPoint and Excel

A **chart** can be inserted inside a content placeholder on a slide in the same way as you insert a picture inside a content placeholder. When you click on the chart icon in the placeholder, you select your chart type and then Excel pop-up screen for charts is opened on top of PowerPoint with sample data. You then replace the sample data with your own information and PowerPoint updates the slide.

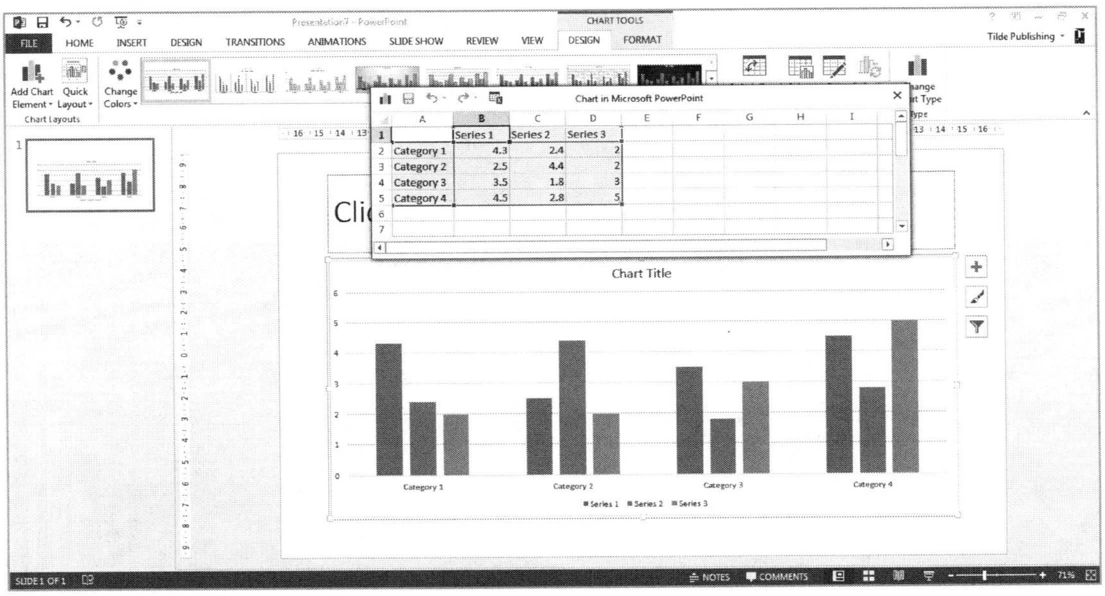

__As an aside__ ... When including a chart don't try to show too much in too little space. If necessary cut back on the data you are showing. Use colours that stand out from the slide background and a font colour that is also easy to read.

How to: Create a chart

1. Add a slide with a slide layout that includes …**Content**.
2. Click on the **Insert Chart** icon. The Insert Chart dialogue box is presented.

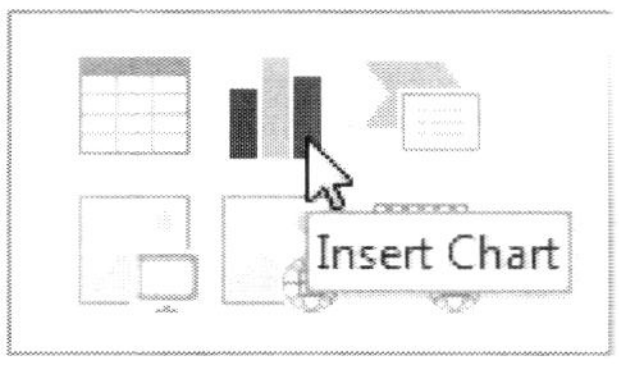

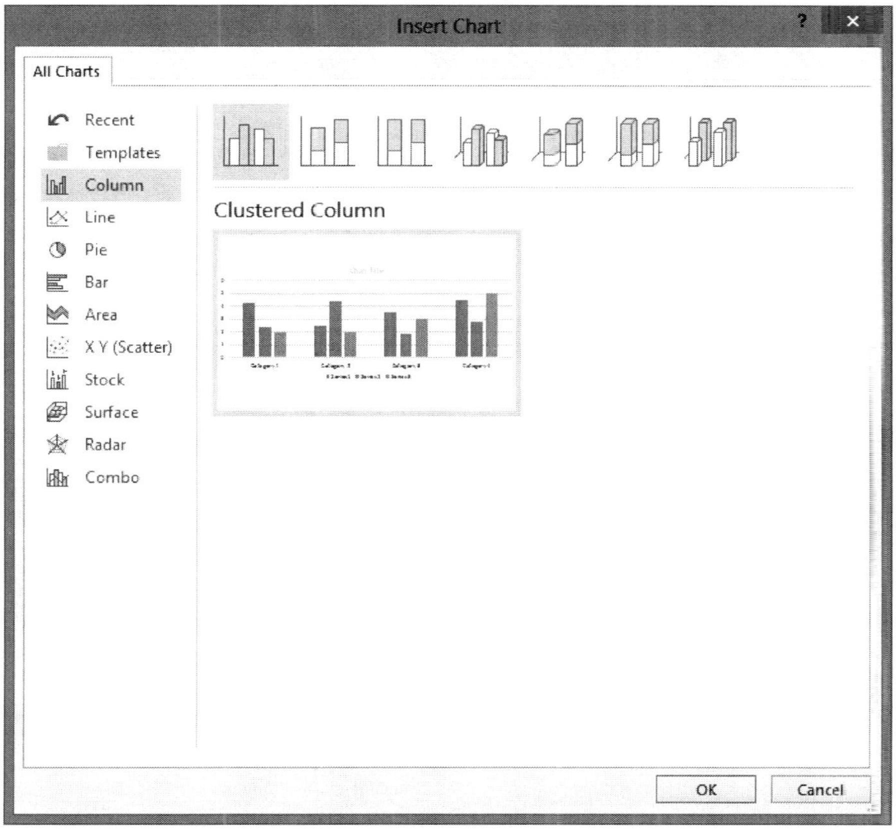

3. Click on one of the charting options on the left of the dialogue box, e.g. Column, Line, then click on one of the chart styles from right of the dialogue box, e.g. Clustered Column.
4. Click on **OK**.
   Excel pop-up screen for charts with sample data will be displayed Your chart is in the PowerPoint slide, and your data is in an Excel worksheet. Two new ribbons are displayed in PowerPoint with Chart Tools (Design and Format). The Design ribbon is active.
5. To replace the sample data in the Excel worksheet, click on a cell and type the new text or numbers required. The chart in PowerPoint automatically updates with the new data.
6. Once you have entered your data, close the Excel pop-up screen.
7. **Save** your presentation in the usual way and the worksheet data is also saved. Closing PowerPoint also closes Excel.

***As an aside** … You can also add a chart to a slide freeform by using the **Chart** button (Insert ribbon, Illustrations group).*

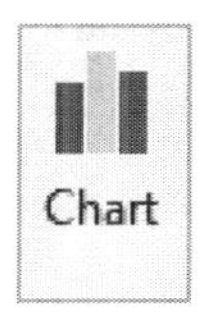

Hands-on exercise 29

In this exercise you practise creating a chart to present numerical data on a slide.

- **Open** the presentation *Gardens illustrated*.
- Display slide 3.
- Click on the **Insert Chart** icon. The Insert Chart dialogue box is presented.
- Ensure the option **Column** is selected on the left of the dialogue box, then ensure the first option **Clustered Column** is selected from right of the dialogue box.
- Click on **OK**.
  PowerPoint and Excel tile side-by-side with sample data. Your chart is in the PowerPoint slide, and your data is in an Excel worksheet.
  Two new ribbons are displayed in PowerPoint with Chart Tools (Design and Format). The Design ribbon is active.
- To replace the sample data in the worksheet, click in the required cell and type the new data. Press Tab to move to the next cell. Type the following data (note how the chart also develops):

Chart in Microsoft PowerPoint

	A	B	C	D	E	F
1		North	South	East	West	
2	Qtr 1	123	235	345	567	
3	Qtr 2	234	345	435	456	
4	Qtr 3	134	234	426	589	
5	Qtr 4	234	567	368	570	
6						
7						

- Your chart is complete.
- Close your Excel pop-up screen.
- **Save** your changes.
- Click on slide 1.
- **Preview** your presentation.
- **Close** your presentation.

Hands-on exercise 30

In this exercise you experiment further with charts in PowerPoint.

- Create a **new** blank presentation.
- Change the slide layout to **Title and Content**.
- Click on the title placeholder, then type: Recycling Profits
- Click on the **Insert Chart** icon. The Insert Chart dialogue box is presented.

- Click on the option **Bar** on the left of the dialogue box, then ensure the first option **Clustered Bar** is selected from right of the dialogue box.
- Click on **OK**.
- Type the following into the datasheet:

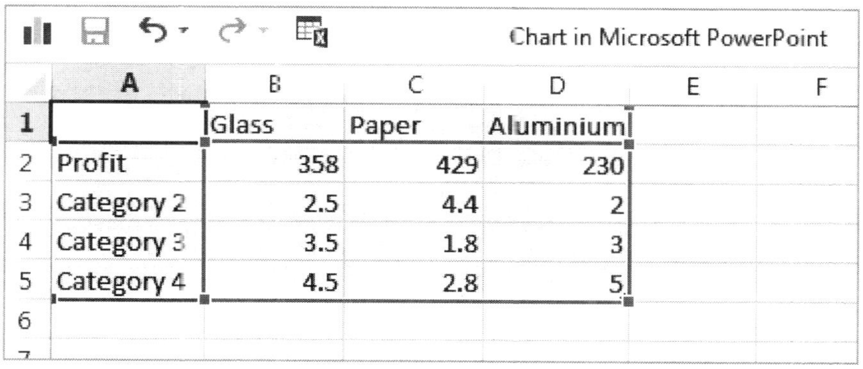

	A	B	C	D	E	F
1		Glass	Paper	Aluminium		
2	Profit	358	429	230		
3	Category 2	2.5	4.4	2		
4	Category 3	3.5	1.8	3		
5	Category 4	4.5	2.8	5		
6						

- To reduce the data plotted on the chart, point to bottom-right corner of the blue defining border. Your mouse pointer becomes a two-way arrow. Drag up so that only the first two rows are selected.

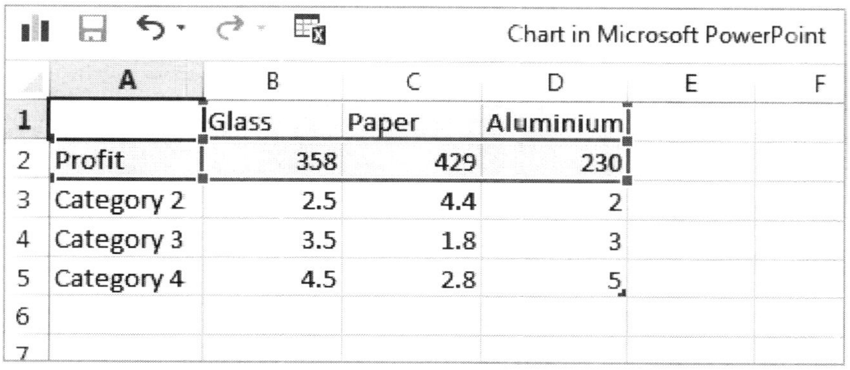

	A	B	C	D	E	F
1		Glass	Paper	Aluminium		
2	Profit	358	429	230		
3	Category 2	2.5	4.4	2		
4	Category 3	3.5	1.8	3		
5	Category 4	4.5	2.8	5		
6						

- Note the effect in your chart.
- Close the Excel pop-up window.
- Click on the *Chart title* and type over the text with the chart title: *Sales from the last 4 Quarters*
- **Save** your presentation as *Profits.*
- **Close** PowerPoint.

Selecting a chart type

The chart type selected to present your data is determined by the data itself.

> ***For example …*** *Bar charts and Column charts are good for representing specific quantities, e.g. sales figures by month, temperatures, rainfall; Pie charts are useful for illustrating the proportion or percentage of items to a whole, e.g. revenue by division within a company; Line charts are useful for illustrating the movement of data, e.g. share prices.*

The Insert Chart dialogue box displays numerous chart options, each with a large number of possible variations. The most popular include:

Chart type	When to use
Column	Use to show changes over time or to compare items at different times.

Line	Use to show the movement of data, i.e. trends over time.
Pie	Use with one data series to show the proportion or percentage of each item to the whole.
Bar	Like column charts but display information in horizontal bars rather than vertical.
Area	Like line charts except the area beneath the lines is filled with colour. Use to show total change (of several items).
XY (Scatter)	Use to show scientific data where several data series are plotted against one category.

Hands-on exercise 31

In this exercise you practise matching data to a chart type.

- Which chart type would be most suitable to show specific quantities and changes over time?

  ____

- Which chart type would be most suitable to percentage or parts of a whole?

  ____

- Which chart type would be most suitable to show the movement of data?

  ____

Editing your chart data

Charts can easily be reopened for editing. There are many effective enhancements you can make to a basic chart.

How to: Edit chart data

1. Display the slide with the chart.
2. Click on the chart to activate the Chart Tools.

3. On the Design ribbon, click on the **Edit Data** button (Data group). Excel pop-up window is opened with the data.
4. Edit the data in the worksheet as previously.

How to: Change your chart type

1. Display the slide with the chart.
2. Click on the chart to activate the Chart Tools.

3. Click on the **Change Chart Type** button (Design ribbon, Type group). The Change Chart Type dialogue box is presented.

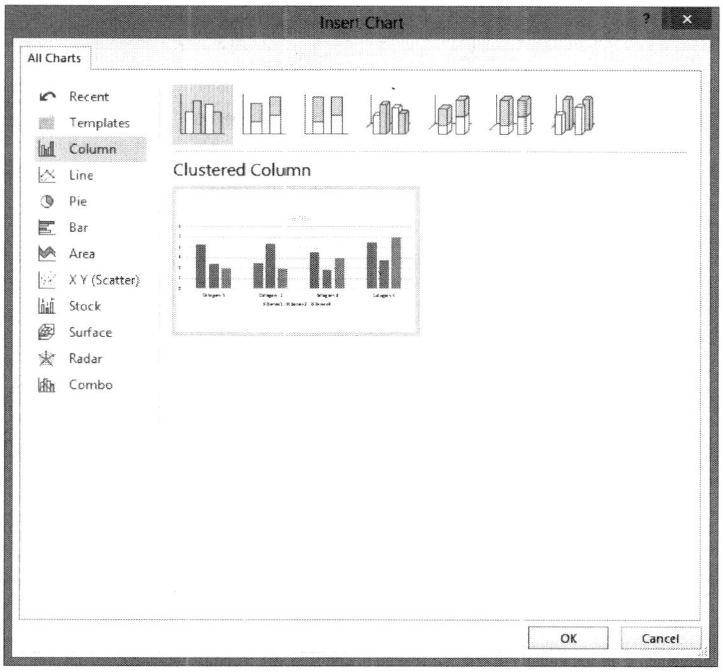

4. Click on the chart type required from the options on the left, then click on a variation from the options on the right.
5. Click on **OK**.
   The chart is updated.

How to: Switch row and column data

1. Display the slide with the chart.
2. Click on **Edit Data** to display the Excel pop-up with your figures.
3. Click on the **Switch Row/Column** button (Design ribbon, Data group).

How to: Apply a quick chart layout

1. Display the slide with the chart.

2. Click on the chart to activate the Chart Tools ribbon.
3. Click on an option in the **Quick Layouts** button (Design/Chart Layouts group).

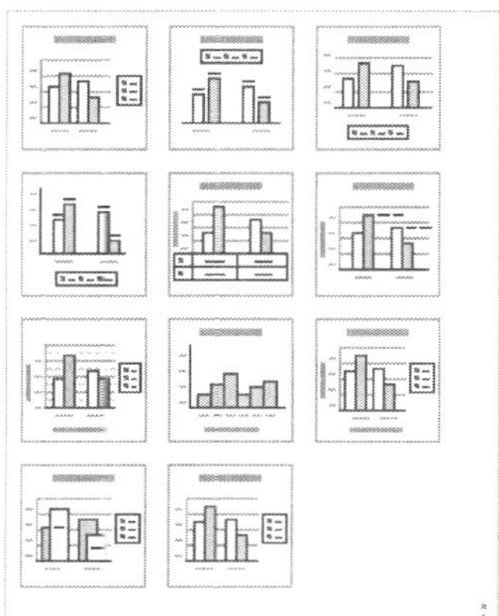

How to: Apply a chart style

1. Display the slide with the chart.
2. Click on the chart to activate the Chart Tools ribbon.

3. Click on an option in the **Chart Styles** group. Click on the **More** arrow to display the full gallery of styles.

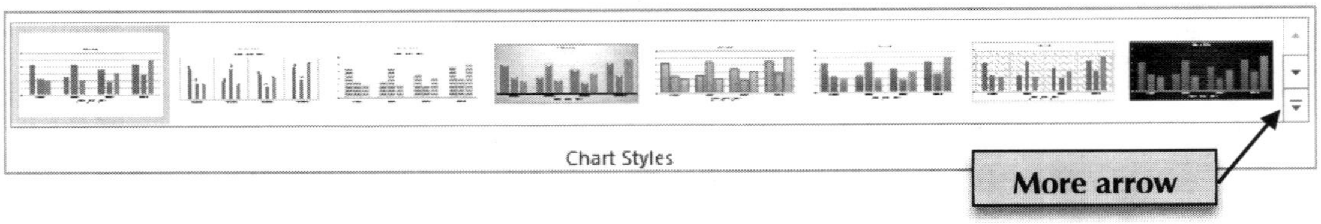

Hands-on exercise 32

In this exercise you practise editing your chart by changing the data and changing the chart type.

- **Start** PowerPoint, and **open** the presentation *Profits*.
  Note Excel is not opened at this stage.
- Click on the chart to activate the Chart Tools ribbon.
- On the Design ribbon, then click on the **Edit Data** button (Data group). Excel is opened.
- In the worksheet, change the Profit for Aluminium to **300**.
- Press Enter. Note that your chart is updated.
- Close Excel.
- Next, you identify some of the areas on the chart.
- Point to the word **Profit** in the chart. What ScreenTip appears?

  ____
- Point to a number running horizontally at the bottom of the chart. What ScreenTip appears?

  ____
- Point to the product Aluminium on the right of the chart. What ScreenTip appears?

  ____
- Point to one of the bars in the chart. What ScreenTip appears?

  ____

Next, you change the type of chart.

- Click on a white area of the chart to ensure no data bars are selected.
- Click on the **Change Chart Type** button (Design ribbon, Type group). The Change Chart Type dialogue box is presented.
- Select **Column**, **Clustered Column**.
- Click on **OK**.
- Display the Excel pop-up window (**Edit Data** button).
- Click on the **Switch Row/Column** button (Design ribbon, Data group).
- **Close** the Excel window.

Finally, you apply a style.

- Apply a style of your choice.
- **Save** your changes.
- Run your **Slide Show**.
- **Close** your presentation.

Hands-on exercise 33

In this exercise you create a pie chart.

- Create a **new** blank presentation.
- Change your slide layout to **Two Content**.
- Click in the title placeholder, then type: Our Wine Exports
- Click in the text placeholder, then type:

  Increased UK exports
  Weak AUD makes our wine cheap in Europe
  Decreased Asia exports
  First year in US market
  Great progress made
- Click on the **Insert Chart** icon. The Insert Chart dialogue box is presented.
- Click on the option **Pie** on the left of the dialogue box, then select the option **Pie in 3-D** (second option) from right of the dialogue box.
- Click on **OK**.
- Type the following into the datasheet:

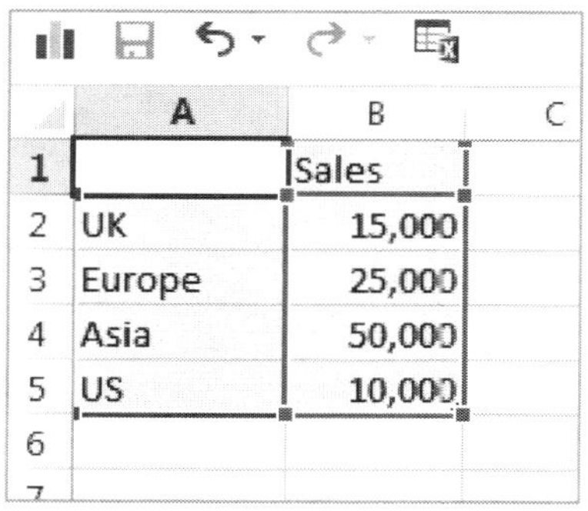

	A	B	C
1		Sales	
2	UK	15,000	
3	Europe	25,000	
4	Asia	50,000	
5	US	10,000	
6			

- Ensure the border surrounds your data.
- Close your Excel screen.
- Apply a **Quick Layout: Layout 2** (Chart Layouts group).
- **Save** your presentation as *Wine exports*.
- Apply the style of your choice.
- Consider widening the text placeholder.
- Review in **Reading View**.
- **Close** your presentation (save when prompted).

Topic 7 – Organisation charts with SmartArt

An organisation chart can be quickly and effectively incorporated into your presentation using **SmartArt**. SmartArt helps you to illustrate information and ideas with shapes, e.g. an organisation chart, steps in a process, cyclical information. In this topic we concentrate on the organisational chart

Creating an organisation chart

An **organisation chart** can be inserted into a placeholder in the same way as a picture or chart.

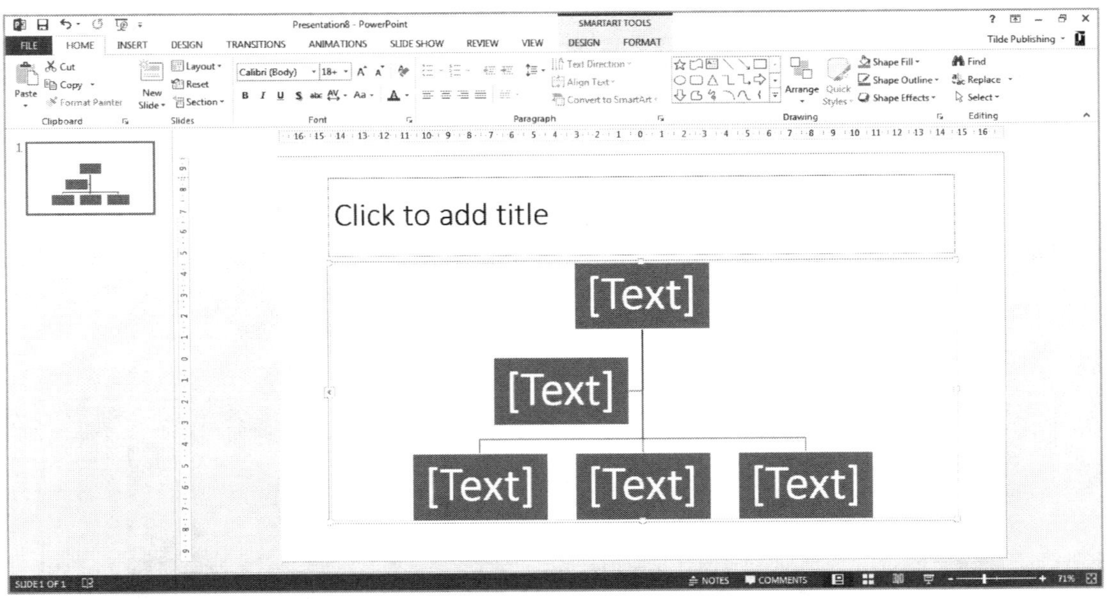

How to: Insert an organisation chart

1. Add a slide with a slide layout that includes …**Content**.

2. Click on the **Insert SmartArt Graphic** icon. The Choose a SmartArt Graphic dialogue box is presented.

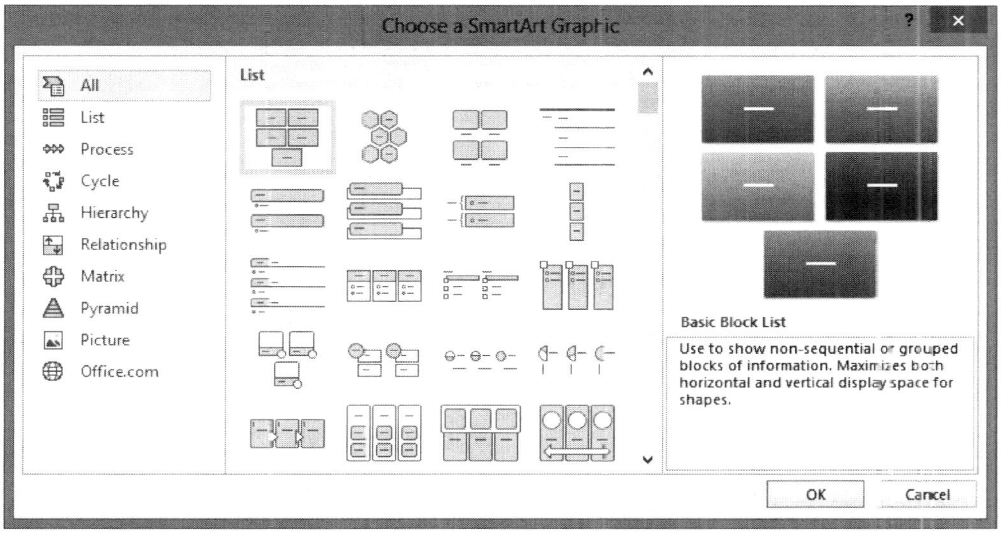

3. Click on the **Hierarchy** option on the left of the dialogue box, then click on **Organization Chart** (first option) from the hierarchy styles on the right of the dialogue box.

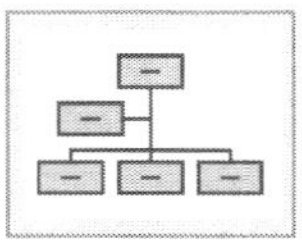

4. Click on **OK**.
   The SmartArt graphic is inserted onto your slide. Two new ribbons are displayed with SmartArt Tools (Design and Format). The Design ribbon is active. Alongside the SmartArt graphic is the **Text Pane**, which can be used as an alternative method to enter text.

How to: Add text

1. Click in a shape (box) box and begin typing *~or~*
   Click on the **Text Pane** button (Create Graphic group) and begin typing. (Your font size adjusts based on the text entered.)

***As an aside** … You can select text and format using Font, size etc. from the Home ribbon.*

Changing the structure and layout of an organisation chart

Organisational charts are arranged in levels, with the "top" level typically being at the top or left of the chart. Once the basic chart has been created, you can change its layout and make adjustments by adding/deleting/moving chart objects.

How to: Insert a shape (box)

1. Click on a box that is on the same level, or a level above or below the box you want to create.

2. Click on the Design ribbon, then click on the **Add Shape** down-arrow (Create Graphic group).
3. Click on the required option.
   - **Add Shape After** inserts a new box to the right but on the same level as the selected shape.

- **Add Shape Before** inserts a new box to the left and on the same level as the selected shape.
- **Add Shape Above/Below** inserts a supervisor or subordinate.
- **Add Assistant** inserts a box below and to the side of the selected box.

4. Add your text.

How to: Delete a shape (box)

1. Click on the edge of the box you want to delete.
2. Press Delete.

How to: Adjust the branch layout

1. Click on the shape at the top of the branch that you want to change.

2. Click on the **Layout** button (Create Graphic group).
3. Click on the required option, e.g. Standard.

How to: Change the chart style

1. Click on the chart.
2. On the Design ribbon, point to any option in the **SmartArt Styles** group to see the design effect previewed on your chart. Click on the **More** arrow to display the full gallery of styles.

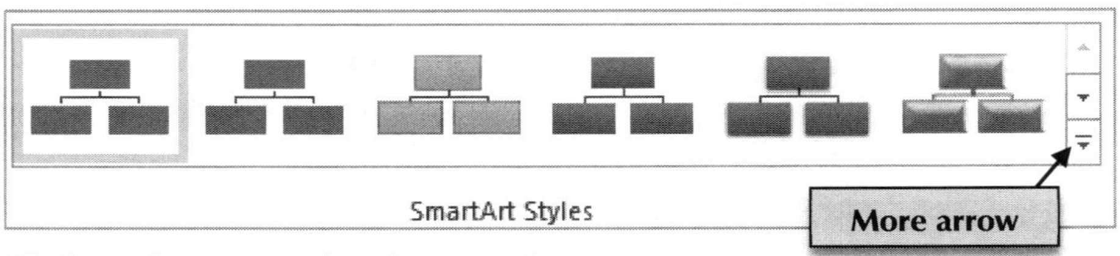

3. Click on the required style to apply.

How to: Change chart colours

1. Click on the chart.
2. On the Design ribbon, click on the **Change Color** button, then click on a colour of your choice.

Hands-on exercise 34

In this exercise you practise creating an organisation chart on a slide.

- Create a **new** blank presentation.
- Change your slide layout to **Title and Content**.
- Click in the title placeholder, then type:
  Our Management Structure
- Click on the **Insert SmartArt Graphic** icon in the placeholder.
  The Choose a SmartArt Graphic dialogue box is presented.

- Click on the **Hierarchy** option on the left of the dialogue box, then click on **Organization Chart** (first option) from the hierarchy styles on the right of the dialogue box.
- Click on **OK**.
  The SmartArt shape is inserted onto your slide. Two new ribbons are displayed with SmartArt Tools (Design and Format).
- Click in the first shape and type: Richard Mortimer
  Press Enter then type the title: Managing Director
- Click in the shape below Richard Mortimer and type: Joseph Hope
  Press Enter then type the title: Special Projects
- Click in the next shape and type: Tim Wallis
  Press Enter then type the title: Finance Manager
- Click in the next shape across and type: Susan Hong
  Press Enter then type the title: Production Manager
- Click in the next shape across and type: James Harris
  Press Enter then type the title: Logistics Manager
- **Save** your presentation as *Management structure*.

Hands-on exercise 35

In this exercise you practise adding to the organisational chart. First, you add further employees to the second level of the chart.

- Using the presentation *Management structure,* click on the **Logistics Manager**.
- Click on the Design ribbon, then click on the **Add Shape** down-arrow (Create Graphic group).
- Click on the option **Add Shape After**.
- In the new shape, type: Sally Lynam
  press Enter then type the title: Sales Manager

Next you create a third organisational level by adding employees below the Finance Manager.

- Click on the **Finance Manager**.
- Click on the **Add Shape** down-arrow, then click on **Add Shape Below**.
- In the new shape, type: Charles Shimmer
  press Enter then type the title: Project Accountant
- Click on the **Finance Manager** again.
- Click on the **Add Shape** down-arrow, then click on **Add Shape Below**.
- In the new shape, type: Jennifer Bridges
  press Enter then type the title: Project Accountant

Now, you change the look of your chart.

- Click on the **Finance Manager** again.
- Click on the **Layout** button (Create Graphic group), then click on **Standard**.
- Add the theme **Integral** to your slide.
- To change the chart style, click on the chart and point to any option in the **SmartArt Styles** group (Design ribbon) to see the design effect previewed on your chart. Click on the **More** arrow to display the full gallery of styles.
- Click on the style **3-D Polished**.
- To change the chart colour, click on the **Change Color** button and click on a colour of your choice.
- With the organisation chart selected, but with no single box selected, display the Home ribbon and change your **Font Size** to 14.
- Return to the SmartArt Tools/Format ribbon and change the **Text Fill** to Black.

Finally, you view your slide as a slide show.

- Review your slide in Reading View.
- **Save** your changes.
- **Close** your presentation.

Hints & tips

What if I want to manually change the size of the shapes?

Resize with the corner/sides sizing handles *~or~*

To make the shapes the exact same size, display the SmartArt Tools/Format ribbon then change the size from the **size** group.

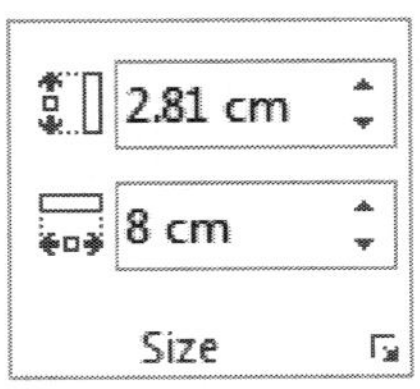

What if I want a different shape to a rectangle?

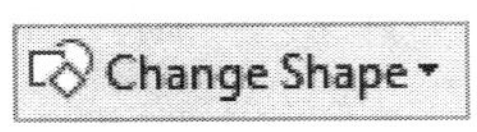

Display the SmartArt Tools/Format ribbon then click on the **Change Shape** button (Shapes group).

Consolidation task 3

In this task you create Organisational Charts to illustrate departments in a company.

- Create a new blank presentation.
- First slide, add a heading: *New Structure for a New Year.*
- Remove the Subtitle placeholder.
- Add an appropriate **Theme** to your presentation.
- On the second slide, create the following organisational chart.

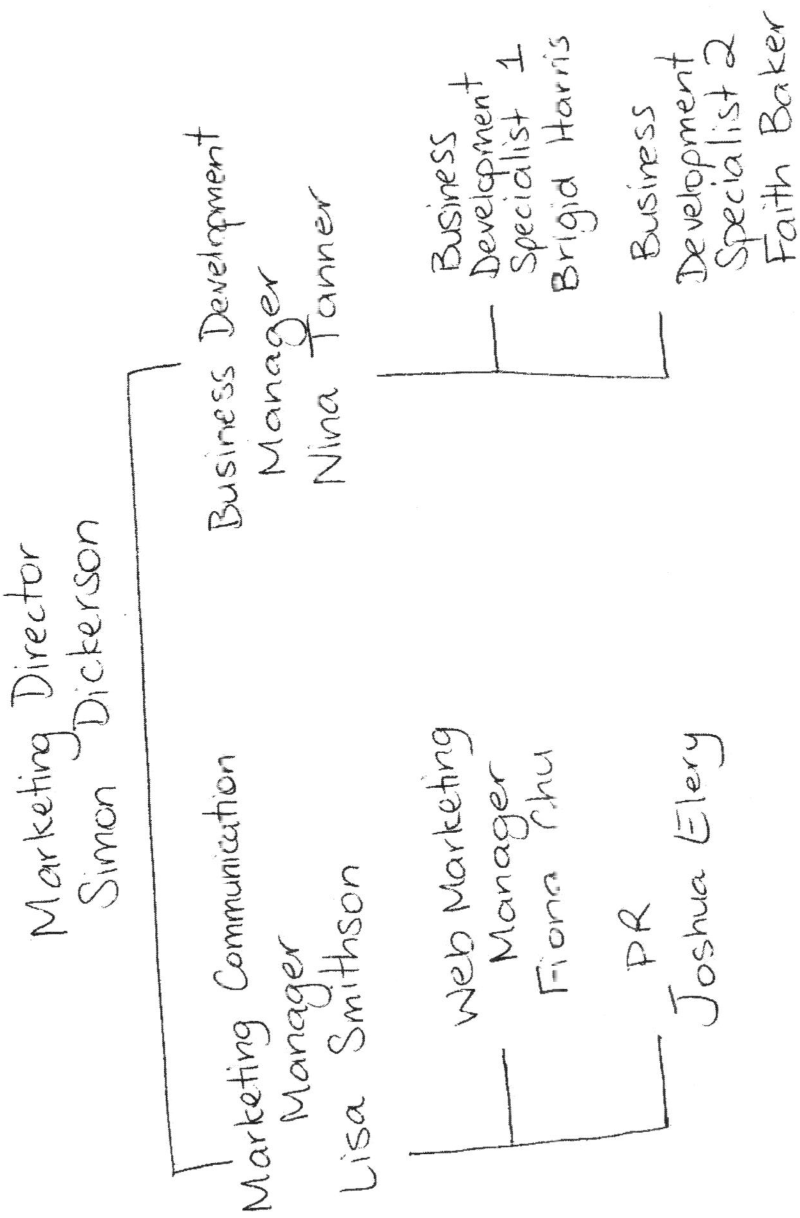

- Format the organisational chart so the positions and names are easy to read. (Hint: Remove the title and make your chart bigger, also see Hints & tips above for changing the size of the shapes.)
- Save your presentation with an appropriate file name.

- On the third slide, create the following organisational chart.

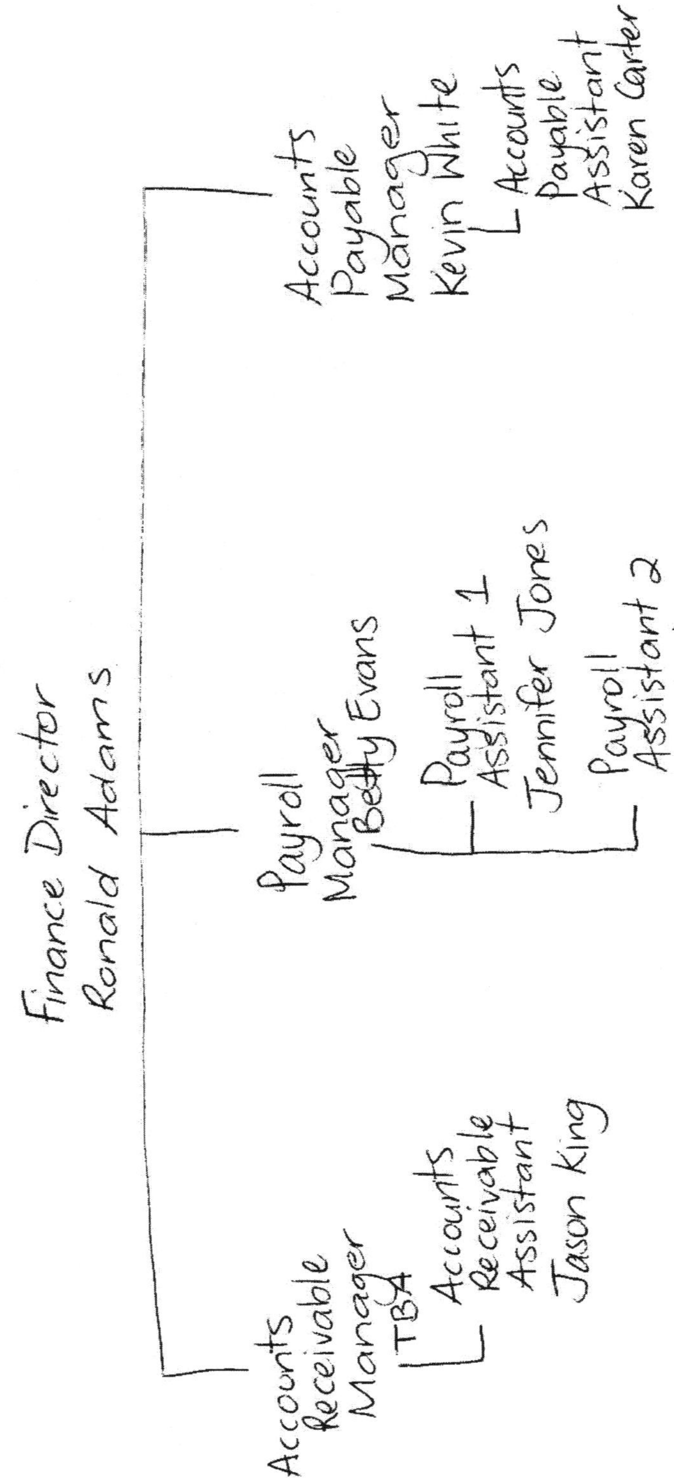

- Format the organisational chart so the positions and names are easy to read and the colour scheme is standard for the two charts.
- On the fourth and final slide, create the following organisational chart.
- Add any SmartArt Styles you think are appropriate (ensure all organisational charts are the same for consistency).

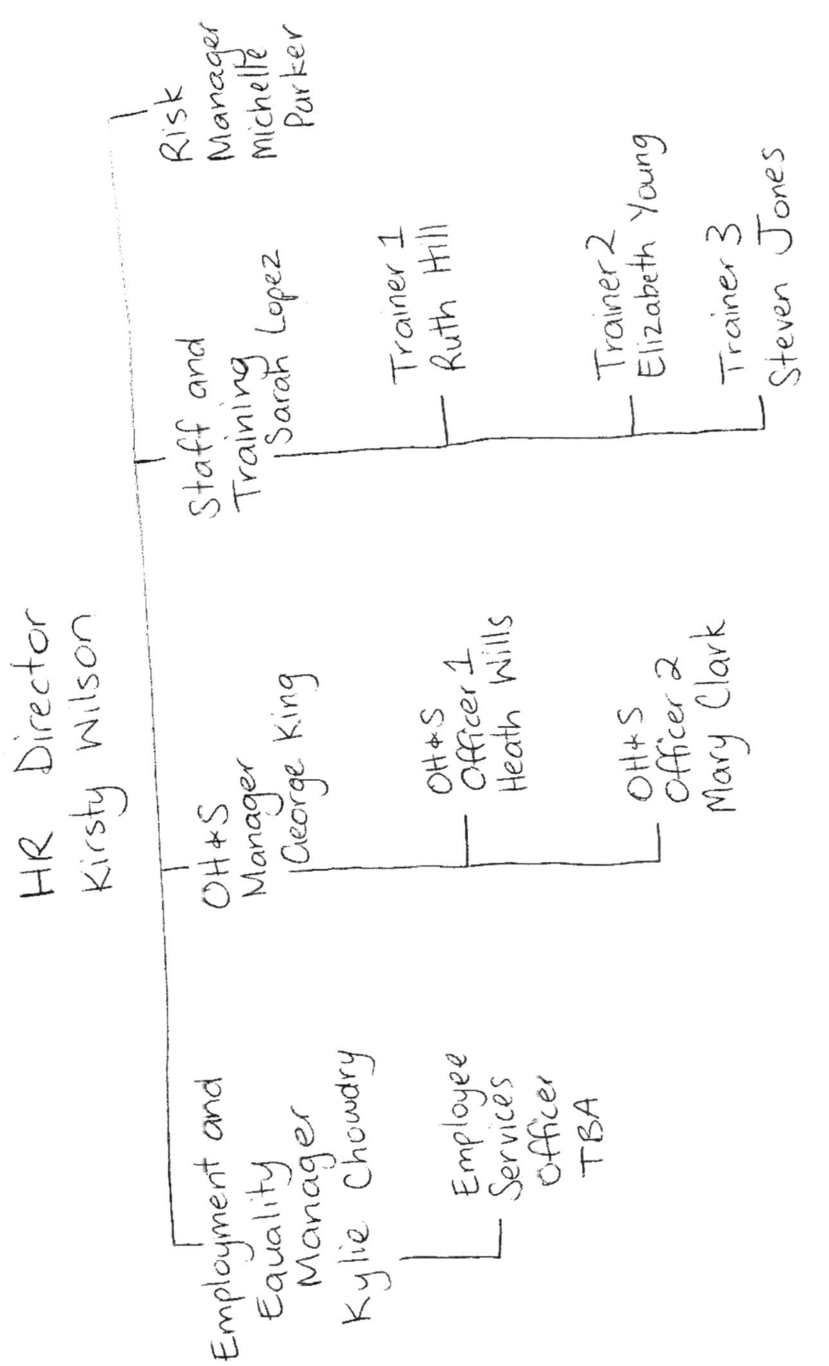

- Format the organisational chart so the positions and names are easy to read and the colour scheme is standard for all of the charts.
- Change the shape for each of the Directors (Marketing Director, HR Director & Finance Director).
- Change the title of Finance Director to: *Financial Director*.
- Change the name of OH&S Officer 1 to: *Heath Willis*.
- Change the position title for Joshua Elery on the Marketing Department from PR to: *Social Media Marketing Manager*.
- Review your presentation and make any changes.
- **Print** your presentation.
- **Save** and **Close** your presentation.

Terms & concepts review

- What are the following buttons used for?

____

____

____

- How do you change the colour of your chart?

____

- Which slide layouts include SmartArt graphics?

____

____

____

____

Topic 8 – Preparing notes, handouts & running your presentation

Final preparations for a presentation may include preparing notes for the presenter and any audience handouts required.

PowerPoint has features that can help you with these tasks. In this topic you learn how to use PowerPoint to prepare **speaker notes** and **audience handouts**.

Then - last but not least - you learn more about running an electronic presentation.

Adding speaker notes

Whether you want to jot down comments about a slide, or add more detailed presentation notes, you can use the **notes pane**. Information entered here does not appear on screen. The notes can be printed separately with a thumbnail of the slide for the presenter's reference.

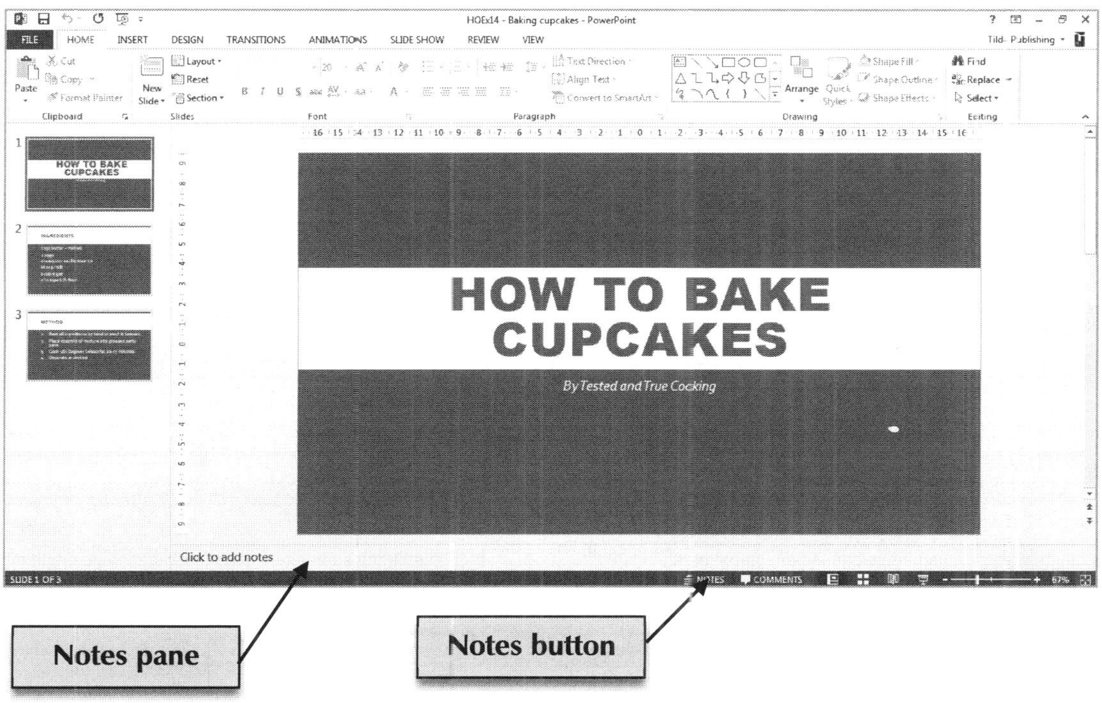

How to: View and enter notes

1. View your presentation in Normal View.

2. Click in the notes button in the status bar.

   ~or~

   Display the View ribbon then click on the **Notes** button.
   Note the Notes pane opens at the bottom of your presentation.

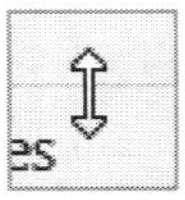

3. You can drag on the splitter bar at the top of the notes pane to increase or decrease its size.

How to: View a full page of notes

1. Display the View ribbon, then click on **Notes Page** button (Presentation Views group). A thumbnail of the current slide is presented with the notes area below.

2. Click on the **Zoom** buttons (View ribbon, Zoom group), then click on **100%**. Click on **OK**.
3. Click in the text area, then type your notes.

How to: Printer speakers notes

1. Display **Backstage** view, then click on **Print**.
2. Click on **Full Page Slides** down-arrow, then click on **Notes Pages**.

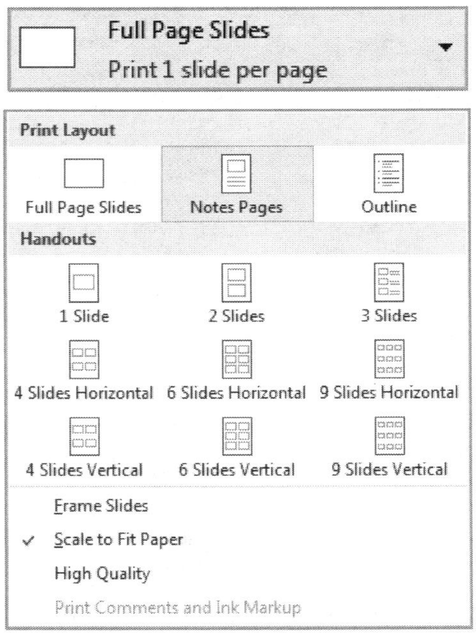

3. Click on **Print**.

Hands-on exercise 36

In this exercise you practise adding speaker notes to a presentation.

- **Open** the presentation *Wave boards*.
- Ensure you are working in Normal view.

First, you want some reminders at the beginning of the presentation.

- Display the first slide.
- Click in the notes pane, then type:

  Introduce myself - credentials.
  Talk about the company and the facilities available.
  Course times, breaks, lunch, equipment.

- Check your spelling.

Next, you add some notes to the last slide.

- Display the last slide.
- Click in the notes pane, then type:

  Close course by reviewing achievements, handing out evaluation forms, and handing out achievement awards.

Next, you review the notes in Notes Page view.

- Display the View ribbon, then click on **Notes Page** button (Presentation Views group). A thumbnail of the current slide is presented with the notes area below.
- **Zoom** to 100%.
- Return to Normal view.

Finally, you print the speaker notes.

- Display the Print screen (**Backstage** view).
- To print the only the slides with notes, click on the **Slides** option, then type: 1,7
- Click on the **Full page slides** down-arrow, then click on **Notes Pages**.
- Click on the **Color/grayscale** down-arrow, then click on **Pure black and white** option.
- **Close** Notes pane in the status bar.
- Click on **Print**.
- **Save** your changes.

> ***As an aside** …Notes has a master where you can set the default appearance for your text. Display the View ribbon, then click on **Notes Master**.*

Using the Handout Master to tailor audience handouts

To help the audience follow your presentation, and remind them of the content later, you can print out **handouts** that contain two, three, four, six, or nine slides per page in either a horizontal or vertical orientation.

You can use the Handout Master to add information to the printed handouts.

> ***For example** … You could add the company logo or presenter's name to each page of the printed handouts.*

How to: Print audience handouts with a header

1. Open the required presentation.
2. Display the View ribbon, then click on the **Handout Master** button (Master Views group).

3. Click into the header box and type the required information.

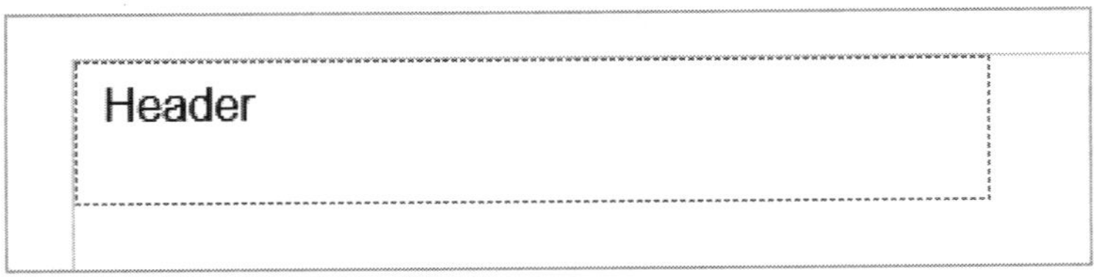

4. **Close** the master.
5. **Display Backstage view**, then click on **Print**.
6. Click on the **Full Page Slides** down-arrow, then click on the amount of handouts per page and the order.

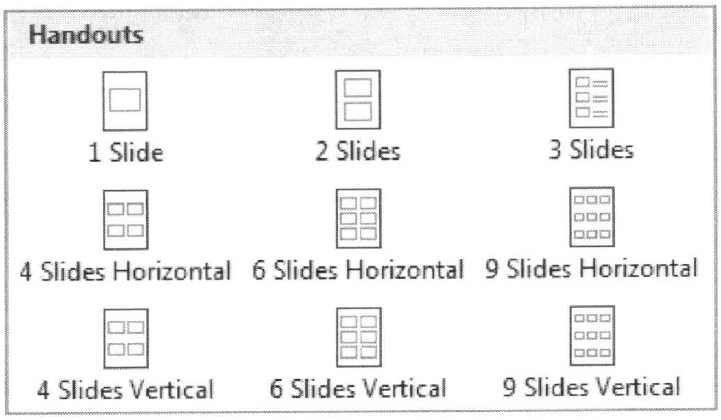

7. Click on **Print**.

> ***As an aside*** *...The three slides per page is a popular handout option as it gives the audience space to write their own notes next to the slide.*

Hands-on exercise 37

In this exercise you practise printing handouts for a presentation.

- Ensure you are working in the presentation *Wave boards*.
- Display the View ribbon, then click on the **Handout Master** button (Master Views group).
- Click into the Header box (top left) and type your name.
- **Close** the master.
- Display **Backstage** view, then click on **Print**.
- Click on the **Full Page Slide** down-arrow, then click on **6 slides Horizontal**.
- Click on the **Color/grayscale** down-arrow, then click on **Pure black and white** option.
- View your handouts in Print Preview.
- Click on another handout option and display in **Print Preview**.
- Finally, click on **3 Slides**.
- Click on **Print**.
- **Save** your changes.

> ***As an aside*** *… If you think your audience will be distracted by handouts during a presentation, don't hand them out until the end!*

Running your slide presentation (manually)

Now it's time to run your slide show with more control.

> ***As an aside*** *…Remember a presentation can be projected from your computer screen to a larger screen using an electronic projector or an LCD panel.*

How to: Run a presentation (reviewed)

1. Display or select the first slide of your presentation.
2. Click on the **Slide Show** button.

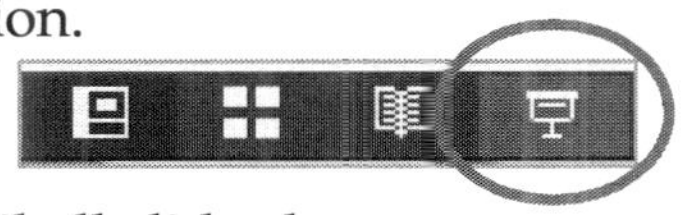

3. Click or press [Enter] to display the next slide until all slides have been displayed and you are returned to PowerPoint ~or~
   Press [Esc] if you wish to stop the presentation.

> ***As an aside*** *… Press* [F5] *to run a slide show from the first slide.*

Useful slide show keys:

Advance to the next slide.	[N] (for Next), [Page Down], [Enter], [Spacebar] or click.
Return to the previous slide.	[P] (for Previous), [Page Up], [Back Space]
Display a black screen (pausing the show), or return to the slide show from a black screen.	[B] (for Black)
Go to a slide.	[slide number] [Enter]
End the slide show	Click to exit, or press [Esc]

Hands-on exercise 38

In this exercise you practise running a presentation.

- Using the presentation *Wave boards*, display the first slide.
- Run your **Slide Show**.
- Click or press [Enter] to progress through the slides. The presentation ends with a black screen. Click to return to PowerPoint.

Next, you run the presentation again experimenting with the additional keys.

- Displaying the first slide, run your Slide Show.
- Click to display the second slide.
- Press [B] to make the slide black, then press [B] again to re-display the slide.
- Click to display the third slide.

- Press P to display the previous slide.
- Type 4 and press Enter to display the fourth slide.
- Press Esc to stop the slide show.

Annotating a slide show

You can use a 'pen' during your slide show to draw on slides to highlight important information.

How to: Create annotations

1. Run your Slide Show.
2. During the presentation, move the mouse and note the buttons that display on the bottom left of the screen.
   Click on the pen *~or~*
   Right-click on your slide show. A shortcut menu appears.
3. Point to **Pointer Options**, then click on a pen and ink option.
4. Draw on your slide, e.g. circle/highlight important points.
5. Press E to **remove** annotations from the current slide.
6. Press Esc to remove the pen.
   Your mouse pointer is displayed again.
7. When you end your presentation the following message is displayed:

8. Respond appropriately.

Hands-on exercise 39

In this exercise you practise using the pen in a slide show.

- Using the presentation *Wave boards*, run your Slide Show.
- Experiment with using the pen to annotate your slides.
- Press Esc to stop the slide show.
- Discard the annotations.
- **Close** your presentation.

As an aside *... To draw a straight line, press* Shift *as you draw with the pen.*

Hiding slides

You can **hide** slides, so that they don't display during a slide show unless revealed. Use hidden slides for supporting details to a companion slide, or for prepared answers to common questions.

How to: Hide/Un-hide a slide

1. Right-click on the chosen slide in the navigation pane, then click on **Hide Slide**.

2. Repeat the above step to remove this feature.

How to: Go to a hidden slide

1. Display the slide before the hidden slide and press H.

Hands-on exercise 40

In this exercise you practise hiding and un-hiding slides.

- Using the presentation *Wave boards*, ensure you are in Normal view.
- Right-click on slide 6 in the Slides tab, then click on **Hide Slide**.
- Run the Slide Show from slide 1 and experiment with showing this slide.
- Unhide your hidden slide.
- **Close** your presentation.

> ***As an aside*** *... Hold down* Ctrl *as you click on the* ***Slide Show*** *button to see your show in the upper-left of the screen. Click away to hide the show; click on* ***Resume Slide Show*** *to return. Press* Esc *to cancel.*

Consolidation task 4

In this task you add notes to the presentation you created in Consolidation task 3.

- Open your saved presentation from Consolidation task 3.
- Add the following notes to the slides.

Slide 2	Welcome Nina Tanner to the Marketing Department. Nina has worked for Zion Marketing for the past 5 years and is excited to be working with us. She has lots of great ideas and is ready to jump in with both feet.
	Welcome Mark Davis to the finance department. Mark completed his course last year and has told me that he would love any hands on experience and open to learning.
Slide 3	We are currently advertising for the role of Accounts Receivable Manager and hopefully will fill this position in the next two weeks. The applicants we have received so far are very encouraging and it will be hard to choose between them. In the meantime, Ronald will be also wearing this hat and filling in where possible while Jason is picking up a lot of the work so if he looks a little stressed, please offer him a cup of tea and assistance where possible.
Slide 4	The HR department this year looks much the same as last year except we now have an opening for the Employee Services Officer. We will be advertising this position in the next month.

- Check your spelling.
- **Print** your presentation to show the slide and notes.
- **Save** your presentation and close.

Topic 9 – Slide transitions & text/object animations

PowerPoint provides an array of effects to make your presentation more interesting and to highlight important information: These include:

- ☐ slide **transitions** (how a slide appears); and
- ☐ **animation** (how elements on a slide appear).

Using slide transitions

You can enhance how a slide appears in a presentation by adding a slide **transition**.

> ***For example ...*** *Your slide can fly in from the top of the screen, or fade in from black. You can also add timings and sound to the slide transition.*

It is important to remember that these features should be used to assist your presentation, to allow a breathing space between slides and to set the tone, e.g. relaxed or fast and snappy. It is recommended that you use one main transition for the presentation, with perhaps the odd slide highlighted with a different transition.

How to: Add a transition to a slide(s)

1. Display the presentation in Normal view/Slide Sorter view.
2. Display/select the required slide.
3. Display the Transition ribbon, click on the **More arrow** button in the **Transitions to This Slide** group to see the full gallery of transitions. Point to a transition option to see a preview on your slide.

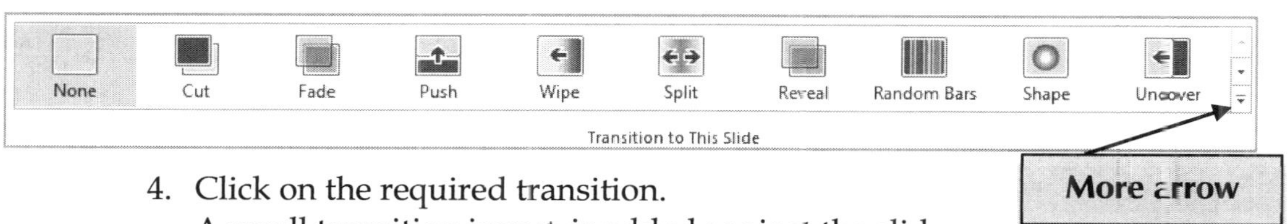

4. Click on the required transition.
   A small transition icon ★ is added against the slide.
5. To set the transition speed, select a time interval (Timing group).

6. If required, click on the **Transition Sound** (Timing group) down-arrow and click on a sound (Transitions to This Slide group).

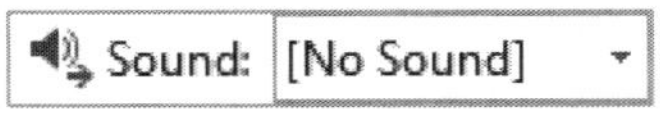

7. If required, click on **Advance Slide: After**, and select a time interval for the advance between slides.

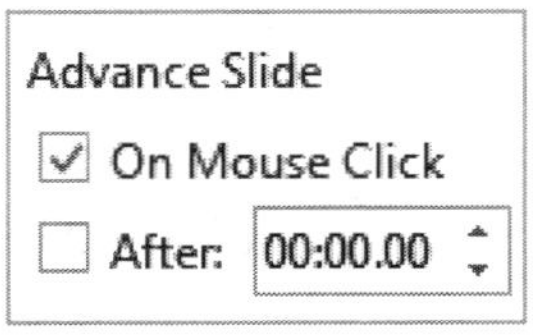

8. Click on **Apply To All** (Transitions to This Slide group) as required.

> ***As an aside*** *... To review a transition on a slide, click on the transition icon ★, or click on **Preview** (Preview group).*

How to: Remove a slide transition

1. Display the presentation in Normal view/Slide Sorter view.
2. Display/select the required slide.
3. Display the Transition ribbon, click on the first option (**None**) in the Transitions to This Slide group.
4. Click on **Apply To All** as required.

> ***As an aside*** *... To select multiple slides on the Slide tab, press* Ctrl *and click on each slide required.*

Hands-on exercise 41

In this exercise you add transitions to your presentation.

- **Open** the presentation *Galaxy boy*.
- Run the Slide Show. The slides currently have no transitions.
- Display the first slide in Normal view.
- Display the Transition ribbon, click on the **More** arrow in the **Transitions to This Slide** group to see the full gallery of transitions. Click on a transition option to see a preview on your slide. Preview a number of options.
- From the Exciting section click on **Page Curl**. A small transition icon ★ is added against the slide on the Slide tab.
- To set the transition speed, select a time interval (Timing group).

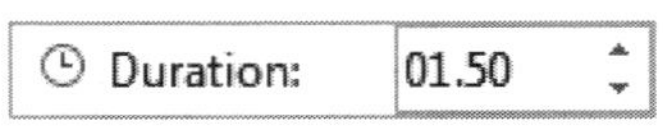

- Click on the **Sound** down-arrow. Preview a number of sounds. Click on the sound **Chime** (Timing group).
- Click on **Advance Slide: After**, and select a time interval for the advance between slides of **00.02.00**. (The default is **On Mouse Click**.)

- Click on **Apply To All** (Timing group).
- Run your Slide Show from slide 1.
- View in Slide Sorter view and note the time against each slide. Return to Normal view.
- To remove the chime, click on the **Transition Sound** down-arrow, then click on **No Sound**, then click on **Apply to All**.
- To remove the timings, deselect the option **Advance Slide: After**, then click on **Apply to All**.
- Run your Slide Show from slide 1.
- **Save** your changes.

Hints & tips

*If you activate both **On Mouse Click** and **Automatically After**, the next slide is shown when the timer expires or when you click on the slide, whichever comes first. If you leave both unchecked you can press the* Spacebar *or* Enter *to progress.*

Adding text and object animations

You can add **animation** options to determine how elements on a slide appear, e.g. showing one bullet point at a time as you click the mouse, or one bar on a chart at a time.

Once again, it is important to use the effects only to enhance your presentation, and not to distract from it.

> ***For example** … Use to stop the audience from reading too far ahead or to save the reveal of an important point.*

How to: Apply an animation

1. Display the presentation in Normal view.
2. Display the required slide.
3. Select the item(s) on the slide that you want to animate. To animate bullet points without a title, select only the placeholder with the bullets.
4. Display the Animations ribbon.

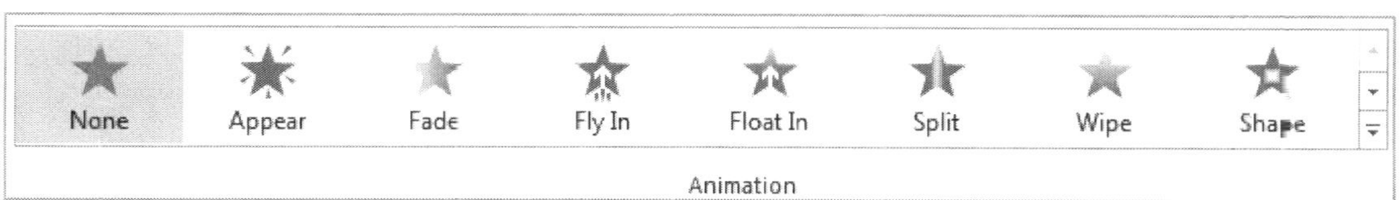

5. Click on the required effect.
   Note the **Start/Direction/Speed** particularly.

> ***As an aside** …If you remove the ability to advance slides on mouse clicks you cannot then animate bullet points on mouse clicks. If you have automatic timings on a slide the time is divided equally among the bullet points, displaying them automatically.*

How to: Change an animation

1. Display the presentation in Normal view.
2. Display the required slide.
3. Display the Animations ribbon.
4. Click on the required effect in the task pane.

5. Click on the **Effect options** button. (Note, the arrow on this button will change depending on the direction of the animation.)
6. Select your new effect.

How to: Remove an animation

1. Display the presentation in Normal view.
2. Display the required slide.
3. Display the Animations ribbon.
4. Select the place holder previously animated.
5. Click on **None**.
   The animation has been removed from the selected text box.

Hands-on exercise 42

In this exercise you practise animating bullet points on a slide.

- Using the presentation *Galaxy Boy*, display the presentation in Normal view.
- Display slide 2.

First, you add animation to bullet points.

- Click on the placeholder with the bullets, then display the Animations ribbon.
- Click on the animation **Fly In** (Animation group).
  PowerPoint previews the effect and the animation details also appear.
- Run the Slide Show for this slide. Click for each of the bullet points to appear.
- Re-display Slide 2 in Normal view.
- Click on the placeholder with the bulleted text.
- The bullets appeared from the bottom of the slide, this can be adjusted.
- Click the **Effect Options** down arrow, then click on the **From Top**.
  Note the preview.

Next, you add animation to a title.

- Still on slide 2, select the title placeholder.
- Click on **Fly In** (Animation group).
- Adjust the **Direction** to **From Top-Left**.
- Note the number applied to this effect (4).

- Run your Slide Show for this slide and note the order.
- Display Slide 2.
- To change the order of the item (4), click on the placeholder then, click **Move Earlier** under Reorder animation (Timing group) to make the title the first animation (1).
- Run the Slide Show for this slide and note the new order.

Next, you add animation to a picture.

- Click on the galaxy boy picture on slide 2.
- Click on **Fly in**.
- Adjust the **Direction** to **From Bottom-Left**.
- Run the Slide Show for this slide.

Next, you remove an animation.

- Ensuring you are on Slide 2, click on item 5 (galaxy boy).
- Click on the **None** button (Animation group).
- Add another animation of your choice.

Next, you add an effect to the chart.

- Display Slide 3.
- Click on the chart.
- Click on **Random Bars**.
- Add animation to the bullet points on Slides 3 and 4. Ensure the bullet points on slide 3 appear before the chart
- Add animation to the galaxy boy on the final slide.
- Run the Slide Show from slide 1 (F5).
- **Save** your changes.
- **Close** your presentation.

Hints & tips

Remember that to avoid annoying your audience, it is a good idea to perhaps pick only one transition and use it throughout your presentation. Then you could use a different transition to highlight special slides, but use sparingly.

If you copy a slide the transition and animations are copied to the new slide.

Remember to use animations only to enhance your presentation, not detract from it. The audience read from left to right, so you might select an effect where the text points fly in one by one from the left. Then, for emphasis on a particular point, you can change the effect and bring the points in from the right.

To add a custom animation to every slide, animate using the Slide/Layout Master. Do this before you start adding individual animations on slides.

Just like charts (graphs) you can add animation to organisation charts.

Consolidation task 5

In this task you create a slide show featuring an organisation chart, a chart, transitions and animations.

- Create the following slides:
    - Slide 1: (title slide): Printers Pty Ltd
      Servicing your printer needs
    - Slide 2: Company Personnel
      Create an organisation chart as follows:

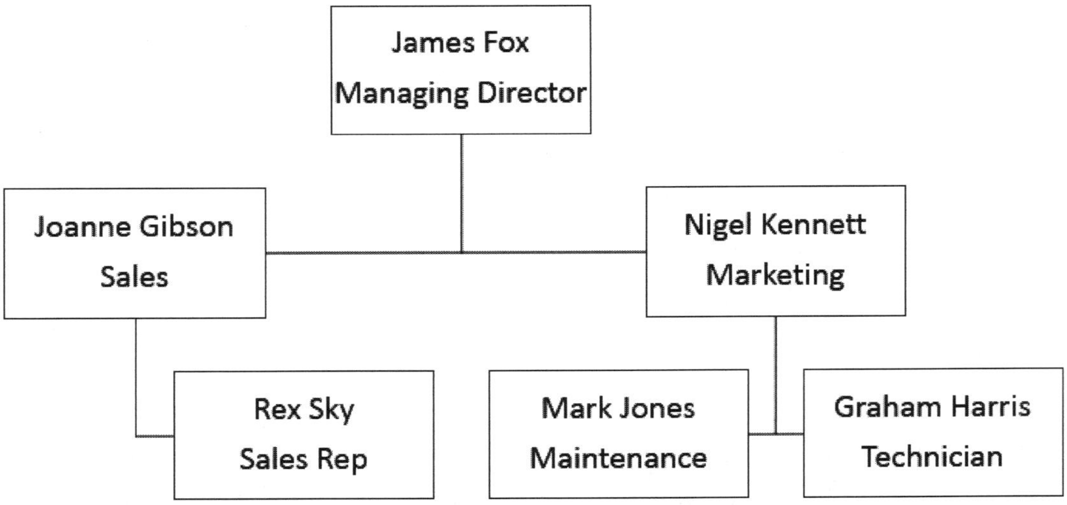

Hint: You made need to change the layout on the Marketing branch.

- Slide 3: Market Leading Products
  Add the following bullet points:

  The Imager
  - -600 dpi
  - -Low noise
  - -Straight paper path

  The Challenger
  - -800 dpi
  - -Whisper quiet
  - -Scanning option
  - -Can receive faxes

- Remember to think about: line spacing, font size, text alignment etc.
- Slide 4: Company Growth
  Create a chart using the following data:

	2001	2002	2003	2004
The Imager	200	400	600	900
The Challenger	100	300	500	700

- Remember to think about chart type, layout, style etc.
- Slide 5: (final slide, display the company motto):
  Printers Pty Ltd "We're here to serve you".

- **Save** your presentation as *Printers.*
- Add a theme of your choice.

- Add a slide number to all slides.
- Make your slide show attractive. Ensure you include appropriate pictures, transitions, timings and animation.
- **Print** audience handouts.
- **Save** and **close** your presentation.

Topic 10 – Rehearsing a presentation

You have seen how to add timings to a presentation using the Advance Slide settings (**Automatically After**) feature. You can also use PowerPoint's timer to rehearse and record time settings.

Rehearsing and recording your timings

When you practice a presentation, PowerPoint can start a timer to keep track of the amount of time you spend on a slide and the whole presentation.

How to: Rehearse for slide timings

1. Display the Slide Show ribbon, then click on the **Rehearse Timings** button (Setup group).
2. The slide show begins and the Rehearsal toolbar displays. The Slide Time box begins timing the presentation.

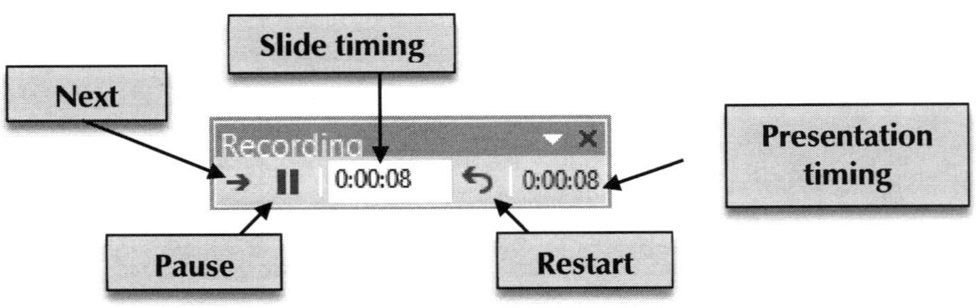

3. Click on the **Next** button when you're ready to go to the next slide. PowerPoint stores the time you take on each slide.
4. When you reach the end of the slide show, click on **Yes** to accept the recorded timings, or **No** to try again. Your timings are noted beneath each slide in Slide Sorter view.
5. When you next run the show, it uses your rehearsed timings.

As an aside *... If you get distracted, click on the* ***Repeat*** *button to reset the time on the current slide. Click on the* ***Pause*** *button to pause, click again to restart.*

Hands-on exercise 43

In this exercise you practise adding timings to your slides.

- **Open** the presentation *Gardens illustrated.*

First, you add a transition and animations to your slides.

- Display slide 1, then add the transition **Drape** (Transitions ribbon, Transition to this slide group) and **Apply to All** slides.
- Change the transition for slide 1 to **Curtains**.
- Choose an animation for the bullet points on slides 2 and 4.
- Run your Slide Show from slide 1.
- **Save** your changes.

Next, you use the Rehearse feature to set timings.

- Display the Slide Show ribbon, then click on the **Rehearse Timings** button (Setup group).
- The slide show begins and the Rehearsal toolbar displays. The Slide Time box begins timing the presentation.
- Click on the **Next** button when you're ready to go to the next slide.
- When you reach the end of the slide show, click on **Yes** to accept the recorded timings.
- View your presentation in Slide Sorter view and notice your timings are noted beneath each slide.
- Run your Slide Show from slide 1.
- **Save** your presentation.

Setting the mode of your presentation

When you run a slide show presentation there are some additional options you can set, such as running your slide show in a continuous loop.

How to: Set the mode of your presentation

1. Display the Slide Show ribbon, then click on the **Set Up Slide Show** button (Set Up group). The Set Up Show dialogue box is presented.

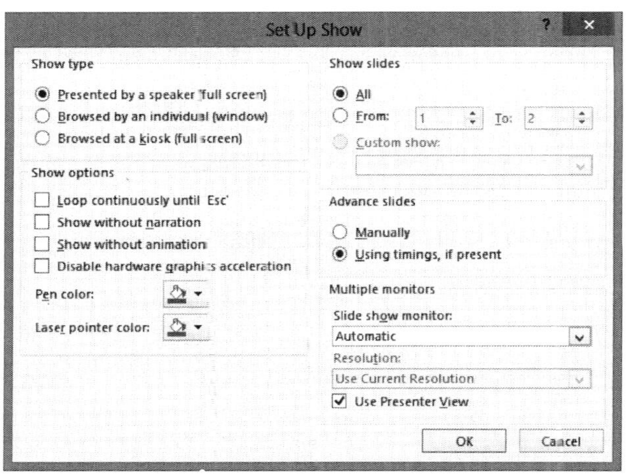

2. Click on the required show type:

Presented by a speaker	This option is the default full screen presentation using the Slide Show button. The show can run automatically or manually.
Browsed by an individual	This option runs the show in a smaller window. This is useful for presentations browsed by an individual over a company network (intranet) or on the internet.
Browsed at a kiosk	This option runs a continuous self looping presentation, e.g. for use at a trade show. This automatically selects the Loop continuously until 'Esc' option.

3. Select any other required option.
4. Click on **OK**.

Hands-on exercise 44

In this exercise you practise setting up a self-running presentation.

- Using the presentation *Gardens illustrated,* set the **Advance Slide: After** option to **00.02.00** for all slides (Transition ribbon/Timing group).
- Display the Slide Show ribbon, then click on the **Set Up Slide Show** button (Set Up group). The Set Up Show dialogue box is presented.
- Click on the option **Browsed at a kiosk (full screen)**. Note that the option **Loop continuously until 'Esc'** is selected automatically (and ghosted).
- Click on **OK**.
- Run your Slide Show and watch it loop.
- Press Esc to stop the show.
- **Save** your changes.

Hints & tips

The pace of your presentation affects audience response. Going too fast can exhaust an audience, while going too slow can put them to sleep!

*A few points to consider when presenting your show on a different PC. Consider selecting **Show without animation** if your presentation is not performing well on the presenting PC. If you know the presenting PC is going to use a different screen resolution, adjust the **Slide show resolution** setting and test.*

*If you are having problems when you turn up at an unfamiliar conference room, go to PowerPoint **Help** and type: troubleshoot.*

Topic 11 – Enhancing your pictures and photos

Enhancing your picture style

A number of effects can be used to enhance your picture style, including:

- applying a picture style
- applying a picture border
- applying picture effects.

There are lots of styles and effects to experiment with.

How to: Apply a picture style

1. Double-click on the picture to select it (and display the Picture Tools/Format ribbon).
2. Point to any option in the **Picture Styles** group to see the design effect previewed on your picture. Click on the **More** button to display the full gallery of styles.

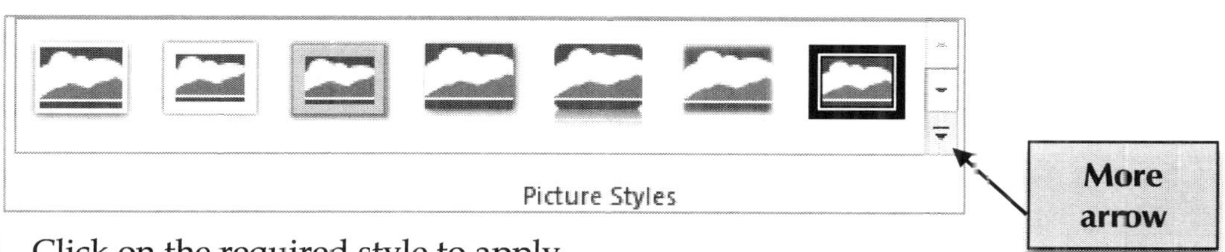

3. Click on the required style to apply.

How to: Apply a picture border

1. Double-click on the picture to select it (and display the Picture Tools/Format ribbon).
2. Click on the **Picture Border** button (Picture Styles group). A number of border colours are presented.

3. Click on the required border colour (note the live preview).

How to: Change the width of a picture border

1. Double-click on the picture to select it (and display the Picture Tools/Format ribbon).
2. Click on the **Picture Border** button down arrow (Picture Styles group).
3. Click on **Weight** and choose the weight of the border. Notice the live preview around the picture.

4. Click on one of the weights.

How to: Add an picture effect

1. Double-click on the picture to select it (and display the Format ribbon).
2. Click on the **Picture Effects** button (Picture Styles group).
3. Click on one of the effects (note the live preview).

Left picture is original, right photo has a picture effect of 3-D Rotation

How to: Add an artistic effect

1. Double-click on the picture to select it (and display the Format ribbon).
2. Click on the **Artistic Effects** button (Adjust group).
3. Click on one of the effects (note the live preview).

Left picture is original, right photo has an artistic effect of Pencil Sketch

How to: Correct sharpness, brightness and contrast

1. Double-click on the picture to select it (and display the Format ribbon).
2. Click on the **Corrections** button (Adjust group).

3. Click on one of the correction options (note the live preview).
   Also note the separate categories Sharpen and Soften, and Brightness and Contrast.

> ***As an aside*** *... Note, if you don't like the changes you have made you can always restore the picture to its original form by clicking on* ***Reset Picture****.*

Hands-on exercise 45

In this exercise you practise enhancing pictures in your presentation.

- **Open** the presentation *Baking cupcakes*.
- Display the final slide.
- Display the Insert ribbon, then click on the **Picture** button (Images group). The Picture dialogue box is presented.
- Locate and insert the supplied picture file from your exercise files folder: *Cupcakes 1*.
- Drag the sizing handles to reduce the size of the picture.
- Drag the picture to the bottom right of the slide.
- Double click on the picture to select it (and display the Picture Tools/Format ribbon).
- Click on the top half of the **Crop** button (Size group) and crop some of the background off the picture.
- Press Esc to remove cropping handles.
- Keeping the picture selected, click on **Corrections** and change the picture to: **Brightness: +20% Contrast: +20** (hover your mouse over the options to see the brightness and contrast numbers).
- Click on **Picture Border** and add a border colour of your choice.
- Change the Border Weight (Picture Border button, weight) to 3 pt.
- Run your slide show from slide 1.
- **Save** your changes.

Adjusting your picture

Again, there are lots of adjustments to experiment with. When removing a background on a simple picture Word can easily remove all in one go, on others you will need to adjust.

How to: Remove a background (adjustments)

1. Double-click on the picture to select it (and display the Format ribbon).
2. Click on the **Remove Background** button (Adjust group).
   Note the new Background Removal Ribbon. PowerPoint colours purple those areas of the picture that it chooses as background and displays an outline around the area to keep.

3. Drag the handles to resize and reposition the rectangle around the part of the picture you want to keep.

4. Refine the areas to keep/remove further by using the **Mark Areas to Keep/Mark Areas to Remove** buttons (Refine group). Click on the required button, your insertion point becomes a pen. Click or click and drag on an area of the picture. Word marks with a + or – sign. Click the buttons again to switch off.

5. On the Background ribbon, click on **Keep Changes** (Close group).

How to: Reset the picture after removing the background

1. Double-click on the picture to select it (and display the Format ribbon).
2. Click on the **Remove Background** button (Adjust group).
3. Click on **Discard All Changes** button.

~or~

1. Double-click on the picture to select it (and display the Format ribbon).
2. Click on the **Reset Picture** (Adjust group).
   Notice the picture has been reset with the background.

Hands-on exercise 46

In this exercise you practise removing the background from a picture.

- Using the presentation *Baking cupcakes*, go to the second slide: Ingredients.
- Display the Insert ribbon, then click on the **Picture** button (Illustration group). The Picture dialogue box is presented.
- Locate and insert the supplied picture file from your exercise files folder: *Cupcakes 2*.
- Drag the corner sizing handles to reduce the size of the picture.
- Drag the picture to the right of the slide
- Double click on the picture to display the Format ribbon.
- Click on the **Remove Background** button (Adjust group).
- Click on the **Keep Changes** button to see what has been cut out of the picture or press Esc.
- Click on the **Remove Background** again.
- Refine the areas to keep or remove by clicking on **Mark Areas to Keep** and/or **Mark Areas to Remove** buttons.
- Click on the **Keep Changes** button to see what has been cut out of the picture or press Esc.
- **Save** your changes.
- Go to slide 1 and display the Insert ribbon then click on the **Picture** button (Illustration group).
- Locate and insert the supplied picture file from your exercise files folder: *Cupcakes 3*.
- Resize and drag the picture to the bottom right of the slide.
- Double click on the picture to display the Format ribbon.
- Click on the **Remove Background** button (Adjust group).
  Note the new Background Removal Ribbon.
- Click on the **Keep Changes** button to see what has been cut out of the picture or press Esc.
- Click on the **Remove Background** again.

- Refine the areas to keep or remove by clicking on **Mark Areas to Keep** and/or **Mark Areas to Remove** buttons. Make sure you can see all the cakes and none of the plate or background.
- Click on the **Keep Changes** button to see what has been cut out of the picture or press Esc.
- Experiment with slide transitions and animation.
- Review your presentation.
- **Save** and **Close** your presentation.

Creating a Photo Album

PowerPoint allows you to easily create a digital photo album. This is a great way to display photos from a recent holiday or to display photos at a farewell of a staff member.

How to: Create a photo album

1. Display the Insert ribbon, then click on the top half of the **Photo Album** button. The Photo Album dialogue box is presented.

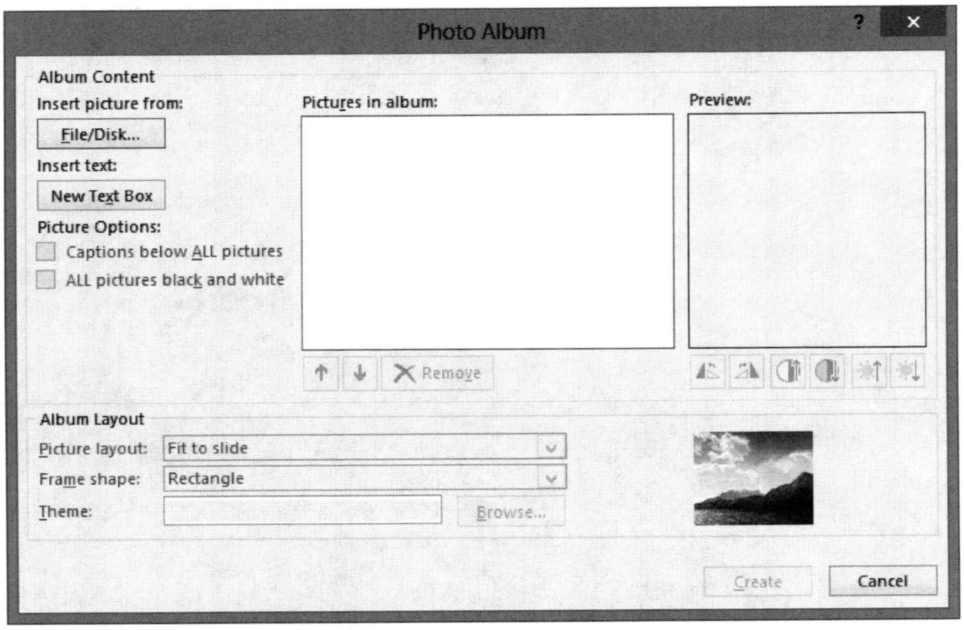

2. Click on **File/Disk...** to import your photos.
3. Locate and select the picture files.
   To select more than one photo at a time, hold the Ctrl key and click on individual files, or for multiple files in a list, click on the first photo and hold down the Shift button then click on the last photo.
4. Click on **Insert**.
   The photos you have imported are now listed in the **Pictures in album:**

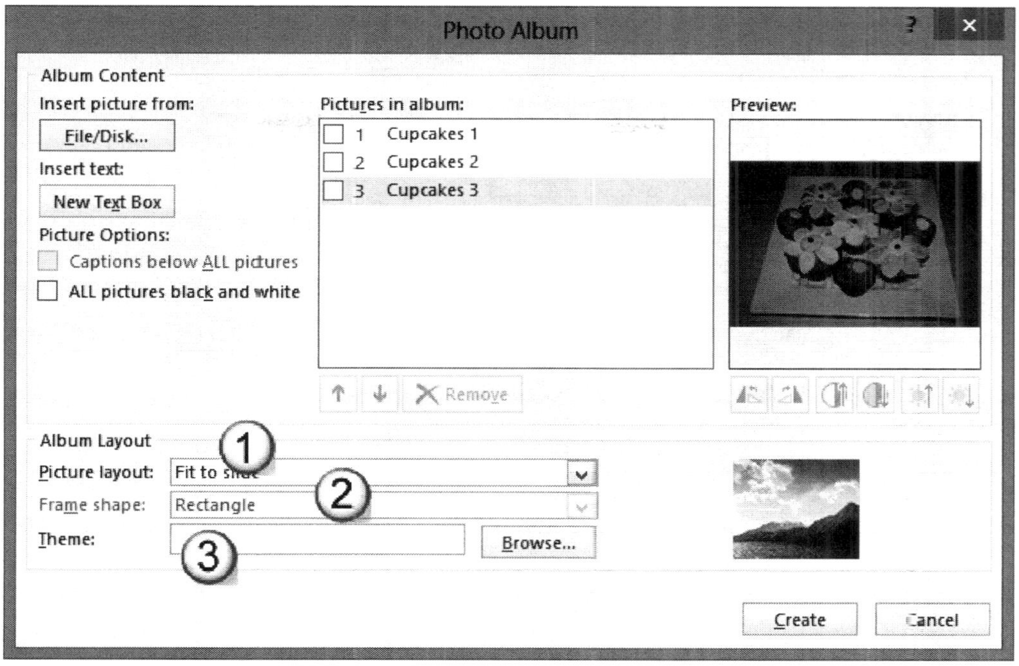

5. Click on the following to adjust the photo album.

Album Layout

1	Picture layout	Select the amount of pictures on a slide.
2	Frame shape	Select the shape of a frame around all the photos (if you require different frames for the photo album, leave as rectangle so it can be changed individually later).
3	Theme	Browse the theme to be used in the photo album (this can also be added at a later point and can be left blank).

Pictures in album:

	↑	Click on the check box for the picture you wish to move up then click on the arrow.
	↓	Click on the check box for the picture you wish to move down then click on the arrow.
	✕ Remove	Removes the photo from the album.
		Rotates the selected picture.
		Increase or decrease the contrast of the picture
		Increase or decrease the brightness of the picture.

6. Click on **Create**.
   Depending on how many photos are in the photo album, it may take a few seconds to open into a new presentation.
7. The photo album is now presented in a new presentation.
8. Give the presentation a title and an author.

Editing your Photo Album

After creating your photo album you may want to add or change some photos.

How to: Edit a photo album

1. Display the Insert ribbon, then click on the bottom half of the **Photo Album** button.

2. Click on **Edit Photo Album...**
   The Photo Album dialogue box is presented.
3. Make any changes needed.
4. Click on **Update**.
   The photo album has been updated to reflect the changes.

Enhancing your Photo Album

A number of effects can be used to enhance your photo album. All the skills learnt earlier in this topic and in Topic 4 can be used to enhance the photo album. Some of these skills include:

- applying a picture border
- applying picture effects
- changing the direction of the photos (rotating and sizing handles)
- recoloring photos.

Don't forget that you can also enhance your photo album by adding:

- transitions
- animation
- themes
- captions to explain the photos.

Ensure your photo album does not become too busy with too many colours and movement.

Hands-on exercise 47

In this exercise you practise creating a photo album.

- Create a **new** blank presentation.
- Display the Insert ribbon and click on the top half of the **Photo Album** button (Images group). The Photo Album dialogue box is presented.
- Click on **File/Disk...** and locate the following files then click **Insert**:
  - *Holiday_1*

- *Holiday_2*
- *Holiday_3*
- *Holiday_4*
- *Holiday_5*
- *Holiday_6*

- Go to *Holiday_3*, click on the check-box then click on the **Rotate** button to put the photo up the correct direction.
- Keeping the *Holiday_3* picture selected, click on the **Brightness** button at least 3 times to increase the brightness of the photo.
- Under Album Layout: Picture Layout, choose **2 pictures**.
- Click on **Create**.
  PowerPoint will open a new presentation with your photo album.
- Browse through your photo album and look at the photos.
- On slide 1, create a heading: *My Recent Holiday*.
- Type your name into *by*.
- Save your photo album as *My recent holiday*.

Next you will change the appearance and add transitions to your photo album.

- Apply a theme of your choice.
- Change the direction of some of the photos in your album by clicking on the photo and moving the green rotating handle to a different angle.
- Apply animations of your choice to your individual photos.
- Apply transitions of your choice to your slides.
- Review your photo album from slide 1.

Next you will add two more photos to your photo album.

- Display the Insert ribbon, then click on the bottom half of the **Photo Album** (Images group), then click on **Edit Photo Album...**
- Click on the final picture in your album.
- Click on **File/Disk...** and locate the following two files:
  - Holiday_7
  - Holiday_8
- Browse through your new photos in **Pictures in album**. Go to *Holiday_7* and click rotate the picture to the correct direction.
- Click on **Update**.
  Notice the new photos have been added to you photo album.
- Change the direction of the new imported photos to reflect the rest of your presentation.
- Review your photo album in slide show.
- **Save** and **close** your photo album.

Consolidation task 6

In this task you create a photo album with transitions and animations.

- Create a photo album with the supplied photos from the folder: *Royal Tasmanian Botanical Gardens*.
- Change settings so there are 2 photos per slide.
- Ensure all photos are all facing the correct direction.
- On the title page, add a title: *Royal Tasmanian Botanical Gardens*.
- Add *your name* as the creator of the photo album.
- Make your photo album attractive (see hints on Page 106).
- Review your photo album and make any necessary changes.
- Save your photo album with an appropriate name.
- Close your photo album.

Terms & concepts review

- How do you change the weight of a picture border?

____

- What effect has been used on the following picture?

____

- What are the following buttons used for?

____

____

Topic 12 – Completing your skills

In this final topic you complete your PowerPoint skill set with a number of useful additional competencies which include:

- importing a text outline
- creating a custom show
- creating a package for a CD.

As an aside *... Note, PowerPoint no longer supports 'save as a web page'.*

Importing a text outline

Text created in Microsoft Word can be **imported** to create a presentation.

For example *... You have been asked to create a presentation based on an existing Microsoft Word report.*

When you import a Word document, text formatted with the style *Heading 1* becomes a title on a new slide. Text formatted with the style *Heading 2* becomes a top-level bullet point, etc. If the source file contains no heading styles, PowerPoint 2013 creates an outline based on paragraphs.

As an aside *... You can also copy and paste text directly onto an existing slide.*

How to: Import a text outline

1. Create a **new** blank presentation.
2. Display the Home ribbon, then click on the **New Slide** down-arrow (Slides group).
3. Click on **Slides from Outline**. The Insert Outline dialogue is displayed with **Files of type** displaying **All Outlines**.
4. Locate and click on the required file, then click on **Insert**.

Hands-on exercise 48

In this exercise you create a new presentation using a file from Microsoft Word.

- Create a **new** blank presentation.
- Display the Home ribbon, then click on the **New Slide** down-arrow (Slides group).
- Click on **Slides from Outline**. The Insert Outline dialogue is displayed with **Files of type** displaying **All Outlines**.
- Locate and click on the supplied Microsoft Word file *Company meeting*, then click on **Insert**.
  Seven slides are imported into PowerPoint.
- **Save** your presentation as *Company progress meeting*.
- Delete the first slide.
- Change the slide layout of the first slide to a **Title Slide**.
- Check that the show set up is: **On-screen show(4:3) (Ensure fit)**.
- Add a theme of your choice.
- Add a transition of your choice to all slides.
- Set automatic timing for all slides to: **00.02.00**.
- Run your Slide Show.
- **Save** your changes.

Creating a custom show

You may have a main presentation that can just be slightly amended for different audiences.

For example *... An audience of board members versus an audience of departmental heads.*

Or you might simply have a long and short version of a presentation and what you present depends upon time allotted or the interaction of the audience.

You can keep all of your slides together in one file but build separate custom slide shows for specific situations.

How to: Build a basic custom slide show

1. Display your presentation.

2. Display the Slide Show ribbon, then click on the **Custom Slide Show** button (Start Slide Show group). The Custom Shows dialogue box is presented.
3. Click on **New**.

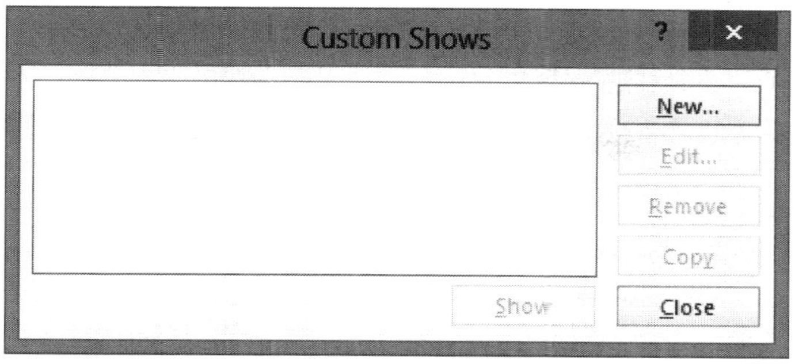

4. The Define Custom Show dialogue box is presented.

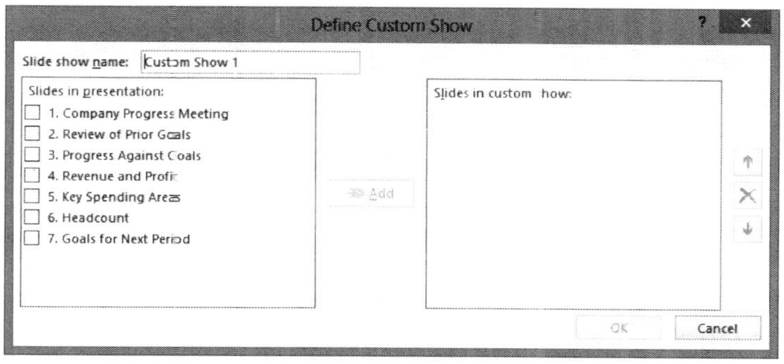

5. Type a **Slide show name**.
6. Select each slide for the show, then click on **Add**.
7. Use the **Up** and **Down** arrows to change any slide sequence.
8. Click on **OK**.
9. Click on **Close**.

How to: Run a custom slide show

1. Display the Slide Show ribbon, then click on **Set Up Slide Show** (Set Up group). The Set Up Show dialogue box is presented.
2. Under **Show slides: Custom show**, select the show required.
3. Click on **OK**. Your custom show is presented.
4. **Save** your changes. (The custom show is part of the presentation.)

Hands-on exercise 49

In this exercise you practise creating a custom show.

- Using the presentation *Company progress meeting*, display the Slide Show ribbon, then click on the **Custom Slide Show** button (Start Slide Show group) then **Custom Shows**. The Custom Shows dialogue box is presented.
- Click on **New**. The Define Custom Show dialogue box is presented.
- Type the following **Slide show name**: Company progress edited
- Select the following slides for the show: 1, 2, 3, 4, 7, click on **Add**. Click on **OK**.
- Click on **Close**.
- **Save** your changes.

- To run your custom show, click on **Set Up Slide Show** (Set Up group). The Set Up show dialogue box is presented.
- Under **Show slides: Custom show**, select the show *Company progress edited.*
- Click on **OK**. Your custom show is presented.
- **Save** and **close** your presentation.

Creating an agenda/summary slide using hyperlinks and custom shows

You can create a slide in a presentation that has links to other slides or custom shows. This slide is often referred to as an **agenda** or **summary** slide.

> ***For example …*** *You are preparing a meeting agenda and have several topics to cover. The meeting agenda is displayed on the first slide. Some agenda items will require two or more slides to be shown (custom show), other topics will only relate to one slide.*

After a custom show has run, the presentation can return to the agenda/summary slide.

How to: Create a hyperlink to an individual slide or custom show

1. Select the text that you want to link.
2. Display the Insert ribbon, then click on the **Insert Hyperlink** button (Links group). The Insert Hyperlink dialogue box is displayed.

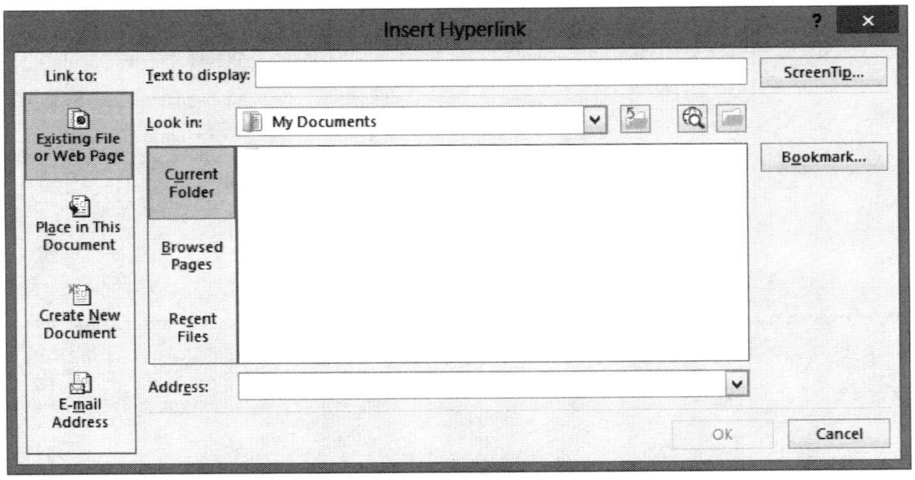

3. Under **Link to:** select **Place in This Document**.
4. For an individual slide, under **Select a place in this document** select a slide under **Slide Titles**

   ~or~

   For a custom show, make a selection under **Custom Shows** (you may need to scroll down to view). Select **Show and return** if you want the presentation to return to the Agenda slide after running the custom show.
5. Click on **OK**.

> ***As an aside** … If you create a link to a **single slide**, the presentation will not automatically return to the agenda slide. You can work around this by creating a custom show containing only one slide and checking the **show and return box** in the Insert Hyperlink dialogue box.*

Hands-on exercise 50

In this exercise you practise creating a meeting agenda presentation.

- **Open** *Soccer Club meeting agenda* and view the Agenda slide, slide 1.

You will use the Agenda slide to run your meeting. The meeting will be run as follows (read this through first then you will be helped with the steps):

i. Slide 1 will be shown and Apologies will be recorded (no separate slide for this).

ii. From the Agenda slide, the convenor will click on **Team selection** and slide 2 will be shown. After this the presentation will return to the Agenda slide.

iii. From the Agenda slide, the convenor will click on **Ground allocation issues** and a custom show will run showing slides 3, 4 and 5. After this the presentation will return to the Agenda slide.

iv. The New rules agenda item will be discussed (no separate slide for this).

v. From the Agenda slide, the convenor will click on **Next meeting** and the presentation will move to the final slide called Next meeting.

First, you create two custom shows, one for **Team selection** and one for **Ground allocation issues**.

- Display the Slide Show ribbon, click on **Custom Slide Show** (Start Slide Show group) and choose **Custom Shows**.
  The Custom Shows dialogue box is displayed.
- Click on the **New** button, and in **Slide show name** type: Team selection
- Under **Slides in presentation** click on **2. Team selection** and click on **Add>>**
- Click on **OK**.
- Click on the **New** button, and in **Slide show name** type: Ground allocation issues
- Under **Slides in presentation**
  - Select slide **3. Watson Oval** and click on **Add>>**
  - Select slide **4. Matheson Park** and click on **Add>>**
  - Select slide **5. Reynolds Oval** and click on **Add>>**
- Click on **OK**.
- Click on **Close**.

Next, you create hyperlinks to the custom shows.

- On the Agenda slide, select the text **Team selection**.

- Display the Insert ribbon, then click on the **Insert Hyperlink** button (Links group).
- Under **Link to** select **Place in This Document**.
- Under **Select a place in this document** scroll down to **Custom Shows** and choose Team selection.
- Check the box **Show and return**.
- Click on **OK**.
- On the Agenda slide, select the text **Ground allocation issues**.
- Display the Insert ribbon, then click on the **Hyperlink** button (Links group).
- Under **Link to** select **Place in This Document**.
- Under **Select a place in this document** scroll down to **Custom Shows** and choose Ground allocation issues.
- Check the box **Show and return**.
- Click on **OK**.
- **Save** the presentation.

Now, you create a link to the **Next meeting** slide.

- On the Agenda slide, select the text **Next meeting**.
- Display the Insert ribbon, then click on the **Hyperlink** button (Links group).
- Under **Link to** select **Place in This Document**.
- Under **Select a place in this document** scroll down to **Slide Titles** and choose **6. Next Meeting**.
- Click on **OK**.

Finally, you test your agenda presentation.

- With the Slide Show ribbon displayed, click on **From Beginning** (Start Slide Show group).
- Click on **Team selection**, the Team selection slide is displayed.
- Click again to return to the Agenda slide.
- Click on **Ground allocation issues**, then click to go to the second, then the third slide of that custom show.
- Click again to return to the Agenda slide.
- Click on **Next meeting** to move to the Next meeting slide.
- Press Esc to finish the presentation.

Hints & tips

If you want to link from one slide to another without returning to the first, you can use the Action button (Insert ribbon, Links group).

Packaging a presentation for a CD

If you have an automatic presentation that can run itself, you might want to distribute it to customers packaged on a CD.

How to: Package a presentation to a CD

1. Display your presentation.
2. Display **Backstage** view, click on **Export**, click on **Package Presentation for CD**, then **Package for CD**.

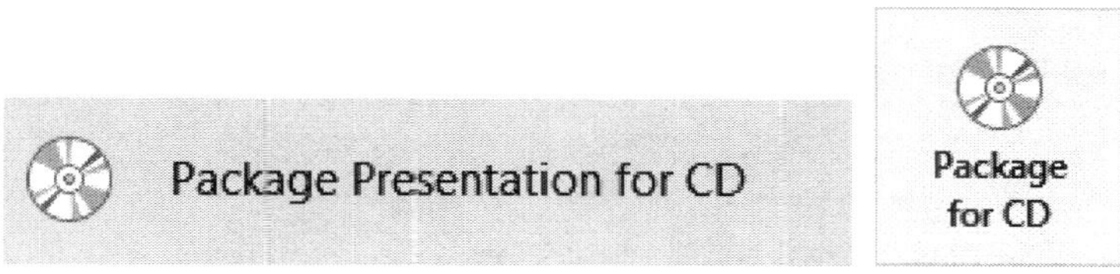

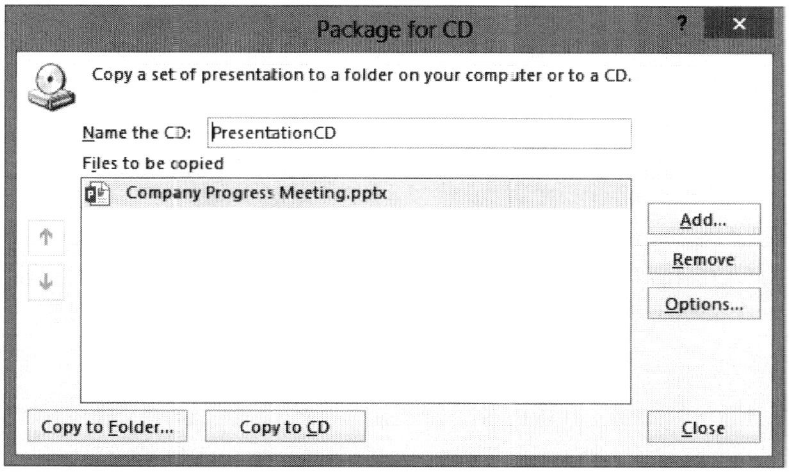

3. **Name the CD** (16 characters or less).
4. The current presentation is included in the **Files to be copied** list.
5. Click on **Options**. The Options dialogue box is presented.

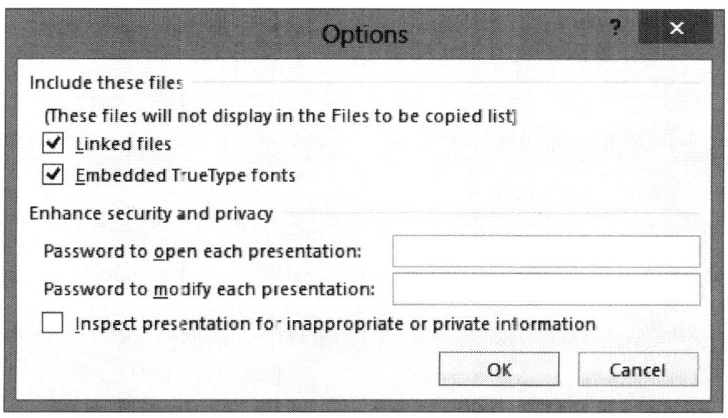

   All presentations are set to play **automatically**. Click on **Embed TrueType fonts** if you have used unusual fonts that may not be installed on a recipient's computer. Add **passwords** if necessary

6. Click on **OK**.
7. Insert a blank CD into your drive, click on **Copy to CD**, then click on **OK**.

Hands-on exercise 51

In this exercise you practise packing a presentation to a CD.

- **Open** the presentation *Gardens illustrated.*
- Display **Backstage** view, click on **Export**, click on **Package Presentation for CD**, then **Package for CD**.
- **Name the CD**: Gardens promo
- Note that the current presentation is included in the **Files to be copied** list: *Gardens illustrated.ppt.*
- Click on **Options**.
  The Options dialogue box is presented.
- Ensure **Embed TrueType fonts** is selected.
- Click on **OK**.

Next, you will create a folder that could be burned onto a CD later.

- Click on **Copy to Folder**. The Copy to Folder dialogue box is presented.
- **The My Documents** folder is selected by default.
- Click on **OK**. Click on **Yes** for the security question, then close the dialogue box.
- **Save** and **close** your presentation.
- **Close** PowerPoint.
- Locate your *folder* in **My Documents (Documents)**. Double-click on the folder to open.

When this folder is burnt onto a CD, the presentation will commence automatically as the CD is inserted into a drive (note the presence of the AUTORUN file). However, for our purposes you view the presentation using the included PowerPoint viewer.

- Double-click on the file *Gardens Illustrated* to launch the PowerPoint.
- Rum your slide show.
- **Close** the PowerPoint and My Documents (Documents).

Skills challenges & Assessment tasks

Skills challenges are undertaken by a student on his or her own, providing further practice and challenges. *Assessment tasks* are suitable to assess competency in the unit.

Creating a working area

Throughout this part of the course you create a number of files. To ensure these are efficiently organised, you need to have a suitable location in which to store them.

The folders needed are: **Commetz** and **Environmental Challenges**. These may be created in **My Documents** or another location as indicated by your teacher or assessor.

If you find you need more assistance with creating folders, refer to the *Managing files and folders* topic in Tilde's *Tilde skills Using Business Technology*. Create these folders before you begin the next section.

Information used in the assessments section was originally provided by Earth Sanctuaries Limited (ESL). Environmental Challenges Australia (ECA) and Commetz Pty Ltd are fictitious organisation.

OH&S

Re-check your workstation setup using your printout of the supplied *OH&S guide* before you continue.

Skills challenge 1

You work in the recruitment and staffing area of Commetz Pty Ltd. You are asked by your manager to prepare a detailed presentation as part of the induction process for a group of new customer service recruits. Text for the presentation can be imported.

You need slides to cover the following topics:

- Company structure
- Mission
- Vision
- Products and Services
- Customer Interface
- Staffing
    - Family friendly policy
    - EEO
    - Conditions

The text can be imported from the file *Presentation text*.

Create a presentation for your manager as follows:

- Import the text file to create a 6 slide presentation, leave the first blank slide.
- Display the first slide and add the title: Commetz and the subtitle: Employee Induction Process
- Use the Spell Check feature to ensure there are no spelling errors

- Save the presentation into the **Commetz** folder using a suitable filename.

The following details some specific style requirements for company presentations:

STYLE GUIDE
▪ Presentation theme: **Retrospect.**
▪ All slides to show a slide number (except the title slide).
▪ No more than one graphic should appear per slide.

- Ensure the style guide points are applied.
- You have been supplied with a number of pictures. Use these in your presentation on the appropriate slides. Size and align the pictures appropriately. (The picture files are: *Mission, Vision, Products* and *Customer interface.*)
- Insert a piece of clip art on the staffing slide. You are only interested in photographs. (Search on words like people, team, etc.)
- The company logo is supplied in the file *Commetz logo* and should appear on the title slide, in the bottom-right corner.
- On a new slide, create an organisational chart to show the company structure. (Use the details from slide 2. You may find this easier if you print out the slide first. The CEO is the top level; the CFO and the Chief of Logistics are the second level; the remainder are the third level. Copy the existing title from slide 2, then delete slide 2. Your new slide replaces the old.)
- Add some presentation notes:
    - for the Products and Services slide, make a note that the Business Review Kits are a recent addition
    - for the Customer Interface slide, make a note that a fast-turnaround email response service is currently being developed.
- Apply a suitable transition and transition speed to **all** slides.
- Review your slide show.
- Add animation to the bullets points on slides 5, 6, 7 so each appears on a separate mouse click.
- Make any other changes to the presentation of your slides or objects on your slides that you think are appropriate and will enhance the presentation.
- Print out audience handouts and notes pages.
- Save your changes.
- Present your slide show to your teacher/assessor.

Skills challenge 2

You are now required to tailor your presentation for use by high level executives joining the organisation.

- Save a copy of your existing presentation to the **Commetz** folder, using a suitable name.
- Create a new final slide.
  The slide will have a title and a chart.
- Type the slide title: *Sales*
- Select a chart type and create a chart using the following data:

	Quarter 1	Quarter 2	Quarter 3	Quarter 4
Sales	$700360	$852639	$698562	$489694
Profit	$565956	$629625	$502634	$298653

- Add some notes to this slide for the presenter on how to use slide annotations.
- Add the title "*Company Overview*" to the header of the Handout Master, then print Handouts with three slides per page.
- Save your changes.
- Present your slide show to your teacher/assessor.

Skills challenge 3

You work in a business cell of Commetz Pty Ltd. You are preparing to chair a staff meeting and want to impress your colleagues by using a PowerPoint presentation similar to the presentation you saw at your induction. The presentation will provide the structure and information for the meeting.

The basic slides for the meeting have been prepared in the supplied file *Agenda*.

- Open the presentation *Agenda*.
- Create an Agenda slide by inserting a new Slide 1 with a line for each section of the agenda. The slide should look like this.

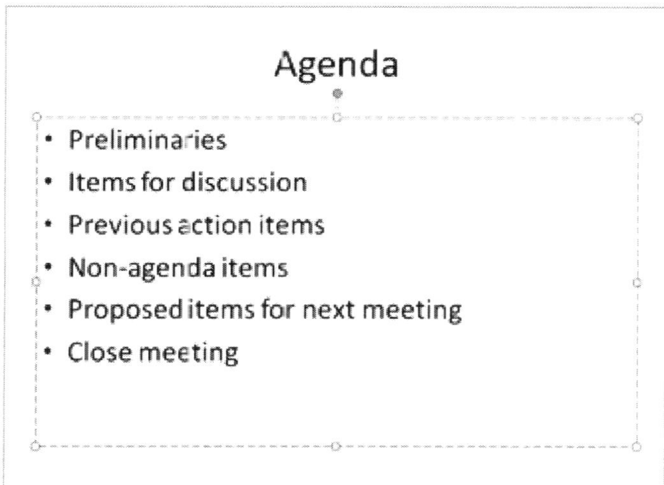

- Create a custom show called **Items for discussion** to show the following three slides:

  - Items for discussion 1
  - Items for discussion 2
  - Items for discussion 3
- Create a custom show to display the **Preliminaries** slide.
- Create a custom show to display the **Previous action items** slide.
- Create a custom show to display the **Proposed items for next meeting** slide.
- Create links on the Agenda slide to link to the custom shows. For each custom show make the appropriate selection so that the presentation returns to the Agenda slide.
- Ensure all slides comply with the company style guide (see **Skills challenge 1**).
- Run the slide show and test that your agenda works as you expect.
- Present your slide show to your teacher/assessor.

Assessment task 1

You work for an environmental organisation called Environmental Challenges Australia (ECA). Your Communications Manager is presenting to a large group of representatives from some major tour operators. The subject is the Margo Bay Sanctuary on Kangaroo Island.

You receive the following voicemail:

Can you create a presentation for me? It is for a group of tour operator representatives. There will be a large audience. We have equipment suitable for an electronic presentation in an auditorium environment. I will need handouts and notes pages. As always make sure you follow company standards!

Thanks.

- Create the following presentation which contains 5 slides.

Margo Bay Sanctuary

Kangaroo Island, South Australia

Ideal Holiday Destination

- Wonderful for nature lovers
- Guided day and nocturnal tours
- 3,485 acres of woodland and paddocks
- Managed wild koala population
- Open all year

Holiday Activities

- Fishing
- Bushwalking
- Pushbike riding
- Swimming
- Canoeing
- Horse riding
- Rafting
- Equipment hire available

Wildlife Wonders

- Koalas
- Tamar wallabies
- Kangaroos
- Insects

- Bats and frogs
- Echidnas

Accommodation

- Bushland setting
- 6 self-contained log cabins
- Great views
- Linen included
- Welcome pack

- Save the presentation into your **Environmental Challenges** folder using a suitable filename.
- Perform a spell check on your presentation.
- Print and proof read your presentation *outline* for accuracy.
- Correct any minor errors and save your changes.
- Ensure your presentation is setup for an on-screen show (4:3).

The following details some specific style requirements for company presentations:

STYLE GUIDE

- Presentation theme: **Retrospect**.
- All slides to show in the footer the following text:
  Environmental Challenges Australia.
  Text to be displayed in the Calibri font, 11 point.

- Ensure the style guide points are applied.
- Run your slide show to review each slide.
- Save your changes.

Assessment task 2

The Communications Manager has reviewed the slides and suggested the following changes:

- Add a new slide after Holiday Activities entitled:
  Visit Us Soon. Apply the slide layout: Title Only.
- Change the layout of the Holiday Activities slide to:
  Two Content.
- Move the following items into the second column:
  'Rafting' and 'Equipment hire available'.
- Rearrange the slides in the following order.
  - Title slide
  - Ideal Holiday Destination
  - Wildlife Wonders

- Holiday Activities
- Accommodation
- Visit Us Soon

- Save your changes.

Assessment task 3

To make the presentation more interesting the Communications Manager has suggested using a few pictures. (These are supplied with your exercise files.)

- You have been supplied with a number of pictures. Use these throughout your presentation including the final slide. Size and align the pictures appropriately. (The picture files are: *Koala, Log cabin, View 1* and *View 2*.)
- Save your changes.
- Review your slide show.

Next, you include the company logo. The logo is supplied in the file *ECA logo*

- Add the *ECA logo* so that it is displayed on all slides. Locate in the bottom-right corner.
- Save your changes.
- Review your slide show.

Assessment task 4

Certain questions may be raised during the presentation on visitor numbers. The Communications Manager asks you to add a chart.

- Insert a new slide after the Accommodation slide (5).
  The slide will have a title and a chart.
- Type the slide title: Visitor Numbers
- Select a chart type and create a chart using the following data:

	Dec	**Jan**	**Feb**	**Mar**
Year 1	1430	1500	1200	1190
Year 2	1490	1567	1300	1389
Year 3	1578	1678	1390	1435

- Review your slide.
- Save your changes.

Assessment task 5

It may also be useful for the Communications Manager to talk about the strength of the management team. He requests another slide with an organisation chart.

- Insert a new slide after the Visitor Numbers slide (6).
  The slide will have a title and an organisation chart below.
- Type the slide title: Key Staff Members
- Insert an organisational chart with the following data:

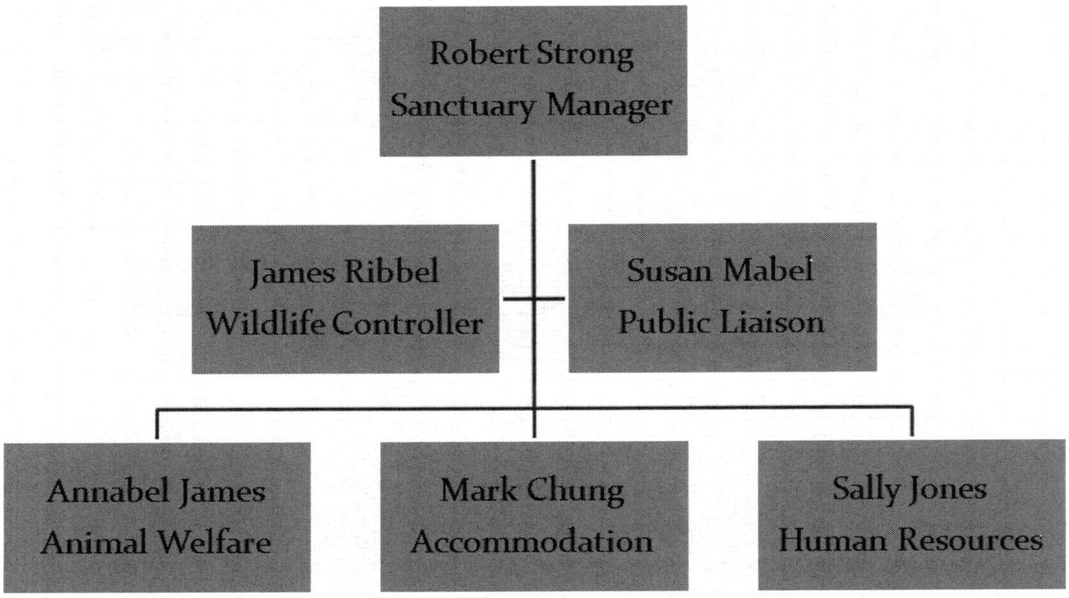

- Review your slide.
- Save your changes.

Assessment task 6

The Communications Manager is now thinking about the task of presenting. He has jotted down some ideas that he wants added as speaker notes.

- Display slide 1 and add the following speaker notes:

  Introduce myself and Environmental Challenges Australia.
  Outline the format of the day.

- Display slide 2 and add the following speaker notes:

  Heritage listed.
  Nature highlights.
  Perfect island getaway.
  Superb accommodation.

- Display slide 3 and add the following speaker notes:

  Discover and learn about wild nature.
  Sustainably managed wild koala population.
  Thousands of trees planted for koala food and habitat – tour costs go towards maintenance.

- Display slide 5 and add the following speaker notes:

  Farmhouse nested in bushland where wallabies and koalas are commonly seen.

- Display slide 8 and add the following speaker notes:

  Lies between Flinders Chase National Park and Kelly Hill Conservation Park, in the south-western corner of Kangaroo Island.

- Hide slide 7 (organisation chart).
- Create a summary slide by inserting a new Slide 2 with the following text:

  Today's Presentation

  - Holiday highlights
  - Wildlife
  - Visitor numbers

- Create a custom show called **Highlights** to show the following three slides: 3, 5 and 6.
- Create a custom show to display the **Wildlife** slide.
- Create a custom show to display the **Visitor Numbers** slide.
- Create links on the summary slide to link to the custom shows. For each custom show make the appropriate selection so that the presentation returns to the summary slide.
- Run the slide show and test that your links work as you expect.
- Save your changes.
- Print out the Notes pages.
- Add the title "Environmental Challenges" to the header of the Handout Master, then print Handouts with three slides per page.
- The Communications Manager will be running the show himself but has asked you to remind him of a couple of basic slide show commands. Complete the following.

  Advance to the next slide.

  Return to the previous slide.

  Display a black screen (pausing the show), or return to the slide show from a black screen.

  Go to a slide.

  Display a hidden slide.

  Annotate a slide.

  End the slide show

Assessment task 7

The Communications Manager has asked you to add some excitement to his presentation, to maintain audience interest.

- Apply a suitable transition and transition speed to **all** slides.
- Review your slide show.
- Save your changes.
- Apply a suitable text animation to titles on the first slide.
- Apply a suitable object animation to the picture on the final slide.
- Make any other changes to the presentation of your slides or objects on your slides that you think are appropriate and will enhance the presentation.
- Save your changes.
- Present your slide show to your teacher/assessor.
- Close your presentation.

Appendix I - Shortcut keys: Direct key combinations

Fundamentals

Action	Keys	Action	Keys
New presentation	Ctrl N	Open presentation	Ctrl O
Close presentation	Ctrl W	Print	Ctrl P
Save presentation	Ctrl S	Save as	F12
Undo	Ctrl Z	Redo	Ctrl Y
Cut	Ctrl X	Copy	Ctrl C
Paste	Ctrl V	Find	Ctrl F
Replace	Ctrl H	Repeat	F4
Spell check	F7	Thesaurus	Shift F7
Move to next pane (normal view)	F6	Move anticlockwise to next pane (normal view)	Shift F6
Switch between tabs in slides/outline pane	Ctrl Shift Shift		
Move down to the next slide	Ctrl Page Down	Move up to the previous slide	Ctrl Page Up

Character & paragraph formats

Action	Keys	Action	Keys
Bold	Ctrl B	Italics	Ctrl I
Underline	Ctrl U	Remove character formats	Ctrl Spacebar
Select all text in placeholder	Ctrl A		
Centre	Ctrl E	Align left	Ctrl L
Align right	Ctrl R	Justify	Ctrl J

Presentations

Action	Keys	Action	Keys
Start a presentation	F5	Redisplay pointer and/or change to pen	Ctrl P
Advance to the next slide or animation	N (for Next), Page Down, Enter, Spacebar or click.		
Return to previous slide or animation	P (for Previous), Page Up, Back Space		
Go to slide 2 (use number of required slide)	2 Enter	Activate selected hyperlink	Enter
Hide the pointer and navigation button	Ctrl H	End presentation	Esc

Display the shortcut menu	Ctrl J	Display a black screen (on/off)	B

Shortcut keys: PowerPoint 2013 access keys

In PowerPoint 2013, you can use an alternative set of key strokes to access ribbons and commands.

How to: Activate access keys

1. Press Alt. Letter badges appear against each tab.

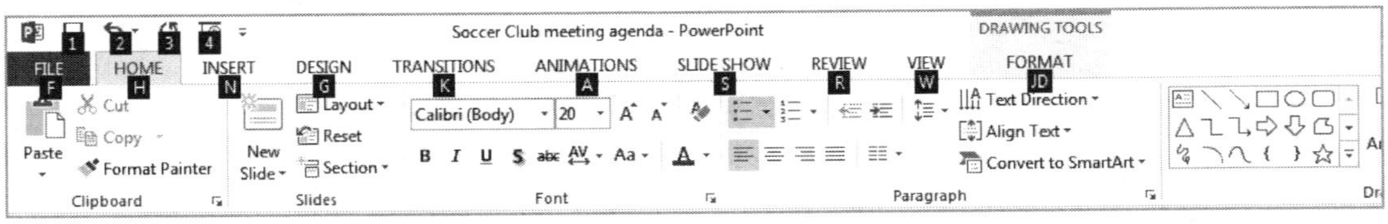

2. Press the required letter to activate a ribbon, e.g. N to activate the Insert ribbon. The selected ribbon is presented with more badges.

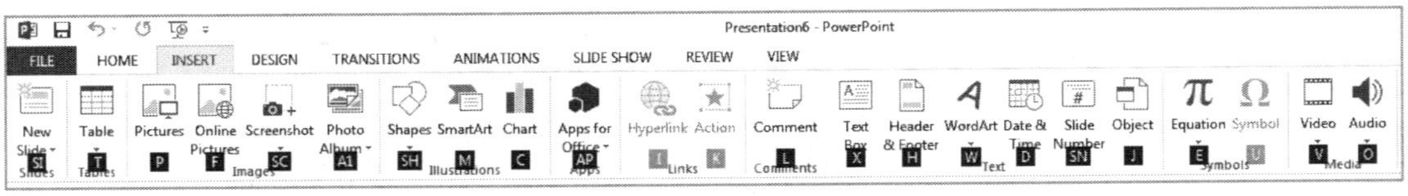

3. Press the required letter for a command. The command is executed and the badges disappear.
4. Once you have memorised these commands, you can simply type them in sequence, e.g. Alt N, P.

> ***As an aside** ...Press* Esc *to hide the badges if you display them accidentally.*

Appendix II – Additional topics

Customising the Quick Access Toolbar

You may find that you have several frequently-used commands that you require quicker access to. Command buttons can easily be added to the Quick Access Toolbar.

How to: Customise the Quick Access Toolbar

1. Right-click on a command button, then click on **Add to Quick Access Toolbar** *~or~*
   Click on the **Customize Quick Access Toolbar** button, then click on the additional commands required from the list presented.

How to: Remove buttons from the Quick Access Toolbar

1. Right-click on a command button added to the Quick Access Toolbar, then click on **Remove from Quick Access Toolbar**.

As an aside *... On the Customize Quick Access Toolbar list, you also see the command Show Below the Ribbon. This is a useful option that brings the toolbar closer to your work and gives you more room to add buttons.*

Using Help

No matter how good your knowledge of PowerPoint, there will be times when you need to look for further information. When you request help, if you are connected to the internet you are connected to online help. If you are not connected to the internet (offline), help files stored on your computer are searched. Online help provides access to extended facilities including tutorials and the latest downloads.

How to: Use Help

? 1. Click on the **Microsoft Office PowerPoint Help** button.

The PowerPoint Help window is presented.

2. Click on one of the links in the Help window *~or~*
   Type a search word or phrase in the **Search list,** [Search online help]
   then press [Enter]
3. If topics are found they are presented in the Help window (as links).
4. Follow the link on the most relevant topic.
5. The following buttons are particularly useful.

   Back

   Forward

   Print

6. Click on **Close** to exit the Help window.

> ***As an aside*** *...To get Help on a particular command button, point to the button until the ScreenTip appears, then press* [F1]. *Also press* [F1] *when displaying a dialogue box to get help on that dialogue box.*

Index

A

Add text to an object, 56
Adding Slides, 21
Align, 57
Animation, 91
  Sound, 93
Animation task pane, 91
Annotations
  Creating, 86
Area charts, 68
Audience handouts, 83
Automating a slide show, 98
AutoShapes, 56

B

Bar charts, 67
Bullets and Numbering, 30

C

Chart types
  Area charts, 68
  Column charts, 67
  Line charts, 68
  Pie charts, 68
  Scatter charts, 68
Charts, 64
  Editing, 68
  Effective use, 2
  Inserting, 65, 74
Close, 15
Column charts, 67
Copy, 35
  Slides, 42

D

Drawing a circle, 56
Drawing a square, 56
Drawing a straight line, 56
Drawing objects
  Add text, 56

E

Electronic presentations
  LCD panels, 1
Equipment, 1
Exit, 15

F

Fit Slide, 10
Fonts
  Effective use, 2
Footers, 40
  Adding date and time, 40
  Adding numbering, 41
Formatting, 26
  character, 26
  paragraph, 28

G

Graphics. *See* Drawing objects or pictures
Group, 57

H

Handouts, 81

I

Import
  Text file, 109
Import Text, 109

L

Layout, 23
LCD panels, 1
Line charts, 68

M

Masters, 38
Move, 35
  Slides, 42, 44

N

New presentation, 20
Numbers
  Changing, 30

O

Online Picture, 49
Open, 13
Organisation charts, 72
Outline view
  Collapse, 44
  Collapse All, 44
  Demote, 44
  Expand, 45
  Expand All, 45
  Move down, 44
  Move up, 44
  Promote, 44
  Show Formatting, 45
Outline View, 43

P

Paste, 35
Picture
  Crop, 53

Recolour, 53
Picture file, 51
Pictures
Effective use, 2, 3
Insert Online Picture, 49
Insert Picture file, 51
Resizing a picture, 52
Rotate, 52
Pie charts, 68
Placeholders, 54
Deleting, 55
Moving, 54
Resizing, 55
Text, 25
Places Bar, 11
Presentation
Running, 81
Presentation structure, 2
Presentation tips, 2
Print
Audience handouts, 83
Printing, 32
Notes, 82
Print, 33
Projectors, 1

R

Rotate picture, 52
Running a presentation, 81
Shortcut keys, 85

S

Save, 11
Quick Access Toolbar, 12
Scatter charts, 68
Slide Master, 38
Slide show
Animation, 91
Annotations, 86
Hidden slides, 87
Options, 97
Shortcut keys, 85, 125
Transitions, 89
Slide sorter view, 41
Slide tab, 42
Slide transition task pane, 89
Slides
Adding, 21
Copying, 42
Deleting, 42
Footers, 40
Moving, 42
Size, 122
SmartArt, **72**
Speaker notes, 81
Spell check, 24

T

Tables, 58
Borders, **62**
Column width, 60
Delete, 60
Insert, 60
Shading, 61
Styles, 61
Task pane
Animation, 91
Slide transition, 89
Text
Import, 109
themes, 17
Toolbars
Outlining toolbar, 44
Transitions, 89
Adding, 89

V

Views
Outline View, 43
Slide show, 85
Slide sorter view, 41
Visual aids, 1